Exploring the Gift of Prophecy

By Steve Condon

Copyright

Published by Steve Condon

ISBN 978-1-9992148-1-4

First printing November 2019

Acknowledgment

I wish to thank all of those who assisted me in completing this book. To those who read through the manuscript, providing feedback, thank you. A heart felt thank you to Jerry, Dorothy, Betty, Reed, Virginia, Mike, Mark, Mary Lynn, Adam, Jordan, John and Dawn for your feedback that assisted me in creating this book to assist others.

To my Pastor, Brian Mahood, thank you for all the ways you encouraged me to follow God on the different path He was leading me.

To my brothers and sisters who believed in me, thank you for your supportive words that helped me believe in the plan God had for me in writing this book.

To Gail, thank you for working through the many pages of the manuscript, giving me good counsel to assemble this book in an enjoyable way to read.

To Serenity, thank you for your assistance in completion of the book cover and the many technical aspects required to make the book available to others.

To Russ and Mave Moyer and their leadership team of EWWM, thank you for the many ways you poured into my life. My journey in the gift of prophecy was activated through you and God drew me quickly because of your prophetic school.

And I especially dedicate this book to my lifelong friend and wife Colleen who was my collaborator and sounding board on the journey of writing this book. Thank you for believing in me and the plan God had for me to complete. You have been a great source of strength to me. Your balanced perspective and supportive nature helped me immensely.

Contents

Introduction

What is prophecy and how do people speak prophetically? How can one hear from God and accurately speak this word to another person? These and other points will be addressed in this book.

I was launched into the gift of prophecy in a church service with no notice. In the middle of a worship song I began to speak out a word in tongues. Fortunately, the worship team leader was keenly aware of what was happening so they stopped singing and softly played the instruments. After a few seconds I spoke out an interpretation in English. This process was uncomfortable for me as I did not enjoy public speaking, let alone speaking for God in public. Several people including the pastor confirmed that what came out of my mouth was from God.

As we walk with God in the gift of prophecy, He will show up wanting to speak through us at times we may find not convenient. We need to become familiar with God and His ways so that we can allow Him to speak through us when He chooses.

Why do we need to know the Word of God if prophecy comes from God? The truth is that God's voice is not the only voice we hear. As a human being we also hear from ourselves, the angelic, the devil and other people in this world. We hear in part and we speak in part words of prophecy that we receive from God. Therefore, it can be affected by the condition of our soul. It is important to have a solid foundation of truth in our lives. This foundation is built on the Word of God through reading and meditating on it. The Word of God is the standard we test all things against. Through regular study of the Word of God we will be able to discern what is true and what is not, what comes from God and what is not supported by His written Word.

People tell me that all can prophesy. Does the Word of God agree with this? We shall explore where the Bible speaks to this and other points of prophecy. As we explore the gift of prophecy, what are the fundamental building blocks needed? How does my personal life impact my flow in the prophetic? We will see that our choices in life have a direct effect on how we operate in this gift.

We will discuss aspects of how a person is launched into the gift of prophecy and how one grows in this gift. I believe God wants everyone to know that He speaks through people prophetically today. For some of you, believing the gift of prophecy is in operation today is a challenge. Although we do not understand everything in the Word of God, we need to believe it is truth.

My learning curve in prophecy has been a vertical one. Some lessons I learned have come the hard way. Many who have gone before us have left a legacy to ease our learning experience. There are many questions people have about the operation of the prophetic gifts in the church today. In this book I will endeavour to address some of these questions and share some things I have learned to make learning easier for you.

The contents of this book will shed light on these and other aspects of prophecy. As I write this book, I ask myself what I could add to the vast knowledge of operating in the prophetic that is not already written. My goal is to share what I have learned about the prophetic as I understand it based on the word of God and my personal experience.

As I write, I am working to convey what God has revealed to me. At times I fumbled my way through the process of learning. It is my desire that as you read through these pages you will experience Aha moments and that you will come to understand how to operate in this wonderful gift as God intended.

Throughout this book I will reference what the Word of God states multiple times through different chapters. This repetition is used to illustrate different aspects of prophecy. I encourage you to ask Holy Spirit to show you the truth as things are stirred in you. Do not allow your current mindset to prevent you from stepping into all God has for you. Allow God to give you new revelation about prophecy, how it operates and the benefits to the body of Christ and to other believers who follow Jesus.

You may have been confused by seeing the prophetic operate in the past. If you were like me, I did not know anyone that would speak such kind words affirming me as a word from God did. You may not have known what to do with a prophetic word when you received it. My hope is you will find answers to your many questions as you read this book.

Embrace this book as an aid to grow in the gift God has for you. May God use the contents of this book to draw you into closer relationship with Him as you grow in the gift of prophecy.

Steve Condon

Chapter 1

Prerequisites to Prophesying

Speaking prophetically for God requires that we are in relationship with Him and filled with His Spirit. The following is an explanation of these requirements for one to speak prophetically.

We must believe God exists and that He wants relationship with us as His children, that He accepts us and receives us where we are in life. Our background, church affiliation or belief system are not a barrier to God accepting or loving us. Although God accepts us where we are in life, He wants us to mature and grow into who He has created us to be.

Scripture tells us, "Repent and be baptized, every one of you, in the name of Jesus Christ for the forgiveness of your sins. And you will receive the gift of Holy Spirit" (Acts 2:38). Before we can speak a word of prophecy, we need our spirits brought to life. This is done through accepting the gift of salvation from God where our spirit is given new life through Jesus Christ. The Word of God says "No one can see the kingdom of God unless they are born again" (John 3:3). It also says "Everyone who calls on the name of the Lord will be saved" (Romans 10:13). To receive the gift of salvation, a person calls on the name of 'Jesus'. You ask Him to wash you of your sin, to save you, to come and live in your heart.

No matter what people claim to be correct, the Word of God will challenge, even offend what we believe. If you feel agitated by anything in this book, recognize that Holy Spirit is at work wanting to shift you out of your current mindset into a more truthful walk with Jesus. The devil knows that once a person calls on the Name of

Jesus his grip on that person will be broken. Therefore, the devil will try to convince you to believe you are already saved because you attend church, you pray to God, you believe in God, or some other religious behaviour. "Salvation is found in no one else, for there is no other name under heaven given to mankind by which we must be saved" (Acts 4:12). The name of Jesus is the only name by which man can be saved. How can we know if we have been saved or not? When a person is saved Holy Spirit shall testify with our spirit that we have been saved and set apart for God. "The Spirit Himself testifies with our spirit that we are God's children" (Romans 8:16). "If you declare with your mouth, Jesus is Lord and believe in your heart that God raised Him from the dead, you will be saved. For it is with your heart that you believe and are justified and it is with your mouth that you profess your faith and are saved" (Romans 10:9-10). If you are not certain you are saved and want to be certain, I have included a prayer to invite Jesus to come and live in you.

Jesus, forgive me. Come into my heart, cleanse me and save me. Be the Lord of my life.

If you have spoken this prayer and believed God's Word, Scripture says you are saved. "Therefore, if anyone is in Christ, the new creation has come. The old has gone, the new is here" (2 Corinthians 5:17). You are a new creation in Christ, a born-again child of God. This means you have been washed clean of all sin, your spirit has been given new life and sealed by Holy Spirit. When you die, you will go to heaven. Walking with God in relationship begins with the gift of salvation. We believe what God said in His Word and respond to it in faith.

There were two thieves that were crucified on either side of Jesus. One of them reached out to Jesus while on the cross. "Then he said, Jesus, remember me when you come into your kingdom. Jesus answered him, truly I tell you, today you shall be with me in paradise" (Luke 23:42-43). We see from this scriptural account that the one thief asked Jesus to remember him when He came into His kingdom. He did not outright ask for forgiveness, yet Jesus forgave him. We know this, for Jesus said, "Today you shall be with me in paradise" (Luke 23:43). We see from this example just how willing Jesus is to forgive us. Even the weakest plea for forgiveness will be heard!

I was made aware of my brother who was in the hospital near death. His health had deteriorated to a point that he lost functionality of his body, including the ability to speak. During a visit, I realized that my brother could still understand what was said. Although he could not speak, God showed me he could confirm yes or no through blinking of his eyes. The doctor's diagnosis of my brother was only days to live. My brother and I had not discussed salvation or what we believe will happen when we die previously. I felt I had to speak to him about accepting Jesus as Saviour so he would go to heaven. I asked my brother, "If you understand what I am speaking to you, blink your eyes to confirm yes." He blinked his eyes. I asked him if he wanted to ensure he was saved and would go to heaven, to blink his eyes if yes. He blinked his eyes. I said a simple prayer asking Jesus to forgive him, cleanse him and save him. I asked my brother, if you agree with this and want to be forgiven, then blink your eyes. My brother blinked his eyes, then a big smile came to his face. I said to him, "You are forgiven and born again as a child of God." God checks the heart of a person so He is able to save a person, even one who can no longer speak. We should not shy away from presenting the gospel because of what we understand. Trust in the goodness of Jesus to forgive a person no matter how they are able to communicate with God. This situation with my brother did not fit my understanding of a person being saved. God showed me that He is able to save a person in spite of their condition or what I understand. This was a valuable learning opportunity for me to learn how God can do what I could not comprehend as a possibility.

In my own life, I was living in a very worldly manner when I heard of Jesus. A sister of mine had spoken to me many times about salvation. Then one time she spoke to me about how I could become a child of God. At the time I was not interested so she left me with a challenge that if I wanted to know more about Jesus to ask Him to reveal Himself to me. I pondered what was said to me for several months. At a low point in my life I chose to call on Jesus. I said, "Jesus, I know I have done wrong, please forgive me. Reveal who you really are to me." My prayer was simple. I did not fully understand what I was saying, but I spoke to Jesus with honest intent.

I did not feel anything happen to me at that moment for I had no idea what might occur. In the days that followed I had thoughts about Jesus come to my mind that enabled me to understand He was God, Saviour and Lord of all. People that knew me noticed my behaviour changing from swearing to speaking about God. As I saw my choices changing, I realized Jesus was at work in my life. I felt compelled to tell people I knew that I had accepted Jesus as Saviour. He had begun His transformation in my life!

Each of us is at a different place on our spiritual journey. Like the thief on the cross we do not know how a person could change their mind in a moment to accept the gift of salvation. We can err in not presenting the gospel message to others fearing it will turn the person off. While respecting others, we need to speak to them about Jesus while they are alive.

God acts in a sovereign manner when He saves people from sin. We need to accept that He will act in ways that do not fit into our understanding. Take for example Saul on his way to Damascus. He was on a mission to destroy the church yet Jesus meets him and saves him. "As he neared Damascus on his journey, suddenly a light from heaven flashed around him. He fell to the ground and heard a voice say to him, Saul, Saul, why do you persecute me? Paul replied, who are you, Lord? I am Jesus whom you are persecuting, He replied" (Acts 9:3-5). In this situation Saul referred to Jesus as Lord on hearing Him speak. Scripture tells us that no one can say Jesus is Lord except by revelation of Holy Spirit. Although Saul only conversed with Jesus, he was saved by Him sovereignly. We should not dismiss people being saved in ways that do not align with our theological understanding.

Being baptized as a new believer is a step of obedience. Water baptism is an outward testimony of the transformation of our life by Jesus. Then Peter said to them, "Repent and be baptized, every one of you, in the name of Jesus Christ for the forgiveness of sins. And you will receive the gift of Holy Spirit" (Acts 2:38). As we enter into water baptism, we are choosing to be marked as a follower of Christ. First, we are marked by salvation, secondly by water baptism. Jesus submitted to being baptized by John the Baptist giving us an example to follow. Through salvation and water baptism we are set apart by God for His purposes in this world. Water baptism symbolizes the death of old nature and rising to new life as a child of God. Being water baptized is a strategic move of obedience for a new believer to take. Through following this instruction, we will receive great blessing. I was saved approximately five years when I decided to follow Jesus into the waters of baptism. While at a service the opportunity was raised by the pastor. He expounded on why it was scriptural and an act of obedience on my part. I choose to obey.

The baptism of Holy Spirit is a gift from God, believers can receive to empower them to do the work of ministry. Jesus said, "If you then, though you are evil, know how to give good gifts to your children, how much more will your Father in heaven give good gifts to those who ask Him" (Matt. 7:11). To receive the baptism of Holy Spirit we must first be saved. We believe what God said about giving the Holy Spirit to His children, so we come to Him, asking to receive this free gift from Him. Pray this prayer to receive the baptism of Holy Spirit.

Father, your word says it is Your desire to give Holy Spirit to all who ask. I want to receive the baptism of Holy Spirit from you. Help me to receive this precious gift from you, I ask in Jesus name.

If you are praying with one wanting to receive the baptism of Holy Spirit, have the person tell God they want to receive the baptism of Holy Spirit according to His promise. Believe what God said in His word that when any two agree on anything they ask for in prayer they shall receive what they ask for (Matt 18:19). Ask the Father to enable them to receive the baptism of Holy Spirit and to speak in other tongues as Scripture states, "All of them were filled with Holy Spirit and began to speak in other tongues as the Spirit enabled them" (Acts 2:4). Often people receive the baptism of Holy Spirit when others lay hands on them & pray with them. However, this is not the only way people receive. We read about how Peter was at the house of Cornelius and Holy Spirit baptized Cornelius and his family without Peter touching them. "While Peter was still speaking these words, Holy Spirit came on all who heard the message" (Acts 10:44). God is sovereign and will move at times, in ways, that do not fit with our theology or understanding.

In Scripture we see there we two distinct indicators that believers were baptized in the Holy Spirit. The first and most important sign was they began to boldly proclaim the gospel about Jesus. We see in Acts 4:23-33 where the disciples were threatened and even beaten, yet they continued to proclaim the message about Jesus, boldly. The baptism of Holy Spirit gave them such courage, they were not intimidated by the threats of physical harm.

The second sign is speaking in other tongues, as the Spirit enabled them (Acts 2:4). When a person receives the gift of tongues, they often receive a few syllables at first. Similar to how a child begins to speak with a few syllables that develop into a language, tongues develop similarly. As the person speaks out in tongues, God adds to their language in tongues. People can receive multiple prayer languages that they can use for different purposes.

Some people have difficulty receiving the baptism of Holy Spirit. Causes of not being able to receive the baptism are; not believing what the Word of God says about the baptism of Holy Spirit, doctrinal conflict, unbelief or human reasoning that believes the gift is not for today. When we accept any belief that is in contradiction with what God's Word says we make God out to be a liar. We can be led into error by incorrectly interpreting Scripture to support our own belief. We do not need to understand all of Scripture, but we must believe it is the Word of God and true. Scripture says that when they were baptized in Holy Spirit they spoke in other tongues as confirmation. The Word of God must be our standard to determine truth. Through the baptism of Holy Spirit God gives us a specific language of tongues for our benefit. We can pray in tongues any time we desire. "No one knows the thoughts of God except the Spirit of God" (1 Corinthians 2:11). Holy Spirit searches the heart of God and so He knows the will of God for us. As we pray in tongues, Holy Spirit gives us utterance to pray the will of God for whom He wills.

I was a believer for many years but had not received the baptism of Holy Spirit. When people asked me why I did not pray in tongues I had no answer, as I did not know. I wanted to, but did not understand why I could not. I later realized I did not understand what the Word of God said about being baptized in Holy Spirit and speaking in tongues. I asked Holy Spirit for help that I could receive this gift. A short time later some friends prayed with me to receive the baptism of Holy Spirit. After praying for a few minutes, one person said, "Start to speak out what is in your mouth." As I did, my new prayer language came out in tongues. I realized I had received the baptism of Holy Spirit and spoke in other tongues as Scripture stated. Scripture tells us become like a little child, so I began to ask innocent questions of God. I took what Jesus said to become like a little child at face value applying it to my life. As I became teachable, God taught me many things. I purposed to include Holy Spirit in as much of my day as I could. As I interacted with Him through my day, He brought amazing growth in me. When I asked Holy Spirit to show me why I had not received the baptism of Holy Spirit He did. He showed me where Scripture states, "You do not have because you do not ask God" (James 4:2). We need to ask Holy Spirit about these things for He wants to be involved in all parts of our life. In my case, I had received the gift of tongues a few weeks earlier but dismissed it. I had been incorrectly taught about the gift of tongues and reasoned what I had received was from the devil. Because of this incorrect belief, I rejected the gift of tongues at that time.

I have included a prayer to ask Holy Spirit to reveal anything hindering you from becoming the person you are called to be.

Holy Spirit, I ask for your help. Remove any lies from my thinking and replace them with truth. Teach me all I need to learn. Help me to receive and understand what you are teaching me, to become who You say I am. I ask in Jesus name. Amen.

We have looked at the scripture requirements for a person to prophesy. I encourage you to begin speaking with Holy Spirit. Express your desire to move forward with Him in the plan God has for you. Ask Him questions to help you move forward, He will help you in every way you need assistance.

Chapter 2

Becoming a Disciple of Jesus Christ

Any person can receive the gift of salvation by calling on the Name of Jesus. The only thing the person must do is ask Jesus to forgive them and accept His gift of salvation. To operate faithfully in the gift of prophecy a person must choose to become a Disciple of Jesus Christ. The following chapter will look at different choices and decisions required to become a Disciple of Jesus Christ.

Our life prior to salvation was like us driving a motorcycle with a sidecar. We rode the motorcycle steering our life as we made decisions, like a person determining the direction of a motorcycle. Our goals were the only goals in our mind. Little thought was given to what God would want.

As we become a disciple, we move from the driver's position on the motorcycle into the sidecar attached to the motorcycle. Like turning over driving of the motorcycle to someone else, we turn over who directs our life to Jesus. Becoming a disciple brings change to how we live our lives. As a disciple we look to Jesus for direction on what He wants us to do. We move from choosing what we want, to doing what Jesus wants.

Once we have received Jesus, we begin the process of discovering our identity as a child of God. Holy Spirit, who now lives on the inside of us, will lead us into all truth, (John 16:13). We learn who God says we are through reading His Word. As we learn to apply what His Word tells us we become more Christ like. In fact the word Christian means little Christ. We discover that God does not need our talent, He wants our submission and obedience to Him.

Each of us must learn to recognize the voice of God. The voice of God we hear is Holy Spirit. As we begin to listen for His voice, we will sense thoughts come to our mind. Other times we will see something in our minds eye or receive a "knowing" about things. To grow in this, we must be intentional, setting time aside to hear what God wants to communicate to us through our day.

As we assign time to listen to what He wants to tell us, we honour Him. As we include Holy Spirit into the events of our day, we will grow in our understanding of Him. As we grow, we begin to understand the instruction He gives us more clearly. We must be intentional in looking to God as our source. People, money and things of this world are resources. When we allow anything other than God to become our Source, we will be loyal to it. This will cause us to shrink back from doing what the Lord asks us to do, afraid of loosing our source.

Jesus said, "I am the vine, you are the branches. If you remain in me and I in you, you will bear much fruit; apart from me you can do nothing. If you do not remain in me you are like a branch that is thrown away and withers; such branches are picked up, thrown into the fire and burned. If you remain in me and my words remain in you, ask whatever you wish and it will be done for you. This is to my Fathers Glory that you bear much fruit, showing yourselves to be my disciples" (John 15:5-8). We remain in Jesus as we read God's Word, apply His Word to our lives, listen to His instruction and obey Him. We bear fruit as we speak with others about Jesus and the gift of salvation that can be theirs.

Holy Spirit is our teacher here on earth. We begin to comprehend that He has so much more for us as children of God, more than we have ever experienced. God accepts us for who we are and where we are when we are saved but does not want to leave us there.

The term dying to our flesh refers to us changing from old patterns of living to new responses to life. We learn these new responses to life as we listen to Holy Spirit as we read God's Word and as we interact with born again believers. "And we know that in all things God works for the good of those who love Him, who have been called according to His purpose" (Romans 8:28). In this passage we read that God works for the good of them, "according to His purpose." When we are faced with situations that we cannot change, we must let go of our own plan and yield our self to God's plan. God is working all things together to bring His plan into being, not our plan.

What does it look like to yield our self to God's plan? We pray that God's will would be done for all parties involved. We ask God to renew our mind, aligning our thoughts with His thoughts. Ask God for help to understand what He is communicating to us. Ask Him for help to respond correctly regardless of the situation.

Through the crucifixion, Jesus prayer was, "Father, forgive them, for they do not know what they are doing" (Luke 23:34). We are to follow Jesus example, forgive and pray for those who hurt us. God will address many parts of our character as a child of God maturing into adulthood. When we are born again our spirit is renewed by Holy Spirit. We discover that old patterns of behaviour and belief systems linger for some time. Dealing with these may require deliverance, inner healing, counselling and a continual washing with the water of the Word of God.

The fruit of the spirit is developed as we make up our mind to stop responding to life as we formerly did but replace those actions with behaviours based on God's Word. Holy Spirit will take us through situations that will cause wrong behaviour traits in us to come to the surface. When this occurs, we need to cooperate with Holy Spirit to see these issues healed. We do this by being honest with how we responded and by asking Him to bring change in us. As He brings this change, He is renewing our mind to think with the mind of Christ, (1 Cor. 2:16, Phil 2:5). As our mind and thinking is renewed, our behaviour will change and we will experience positive transformation from the inside out.

Jesus spoke of John the Baptist that there was no one like him on this earth. As John walked on the earth, he spoke of how he needed to decrease and Jesus had to increase. The forerunner of the Saviour of the world realized Jesus needs to increase in his life. Jesus must increase in our life as well. We allow Jesus to increase as we humble ourselves doing what He calls us to do. We do not pursue recognition for what was done, but give Him the credit.

As a disciple, we are learning to bring our soul, which is our mind, will and emotions under the control of our spirit. At the same time, we want our spirit to submit to Holy Spirit. We need to learn to stop insisting on what we want and learn to do what God asks us to do. Through pushing our own plan and claiming it to be from God, we fool ourselves. No matter how good we make the presentation, our efforts will not win souls for Jesus.

Our obedience to God is a progressive journey. As we go through our life, we will experience times when we feel we are under attack. There will be times that God is challenging our fleshly ways yet we may think it is the devil. To develop our character, God will place us around people and settings that will challenge us. We will benefit much more as we cooperate with what God wants to do. This means we need to accept being in the setting that may not be what we feel is best for us. We may be placed amongst people that we feel are no benefit to us.

Where we are now is our current assignment. We should ask God to help us accomplish the work He has for us where we are. Ask God for wisdom to allow Him to operate through you more easily.

God placed me in a position where I was exposed to sensitive information. He taught me to keep my mouth shut when I was made aware of information that could not be readily shared. This is a character trait that is required in the prophetic as well. Our Father reveals secrets from His heart for someone. Firstly, we should pray and intercede for that person that God specifically puts on our heart. It is necessary to be able to hold on to that information until the time is right to deliver it.

God will use pleasant and unpleasant circumstances to refine our character. A wise question to ask God when in these circumstances is, "Lord, what are you trying to teach me in this"?

God allowed the apostles Peter and John to be questioned by the Pharisees then beaten for obedience to Him. Peter and John were proclaiming the gospel, they did nothing wrong yet they were beaten, (Acts 5:40). God allowed them to go through the questioning and beating to fulfill His purposes. He is at work in every circumstance, no matter how others treat us.

Jesus said a student is not above their master. Character is grown as we refuse to react to the inappropriate behaviour of others. As we work our way through difficult circumstances, character flaws or sin in us will come to the surface. The devil may use our family, our neighbours, our coworkers, or our church family to attack us in some way. Our part is to rise above the behaviour of others and respond in a Christian-like way. To be shaped by all of life's circumstances, to be more like Christ.

When we make choices based upon our feelings we are operating out of our soul. Feelings are not facts but are rather responses to various stimuli such as words, looks or actions. A wise friend has said, "Feelings do not have brains." When we give too much credibility to our feelings, we react to situations rather than deal with them. In order for us to walk in victory we must learn to walk above the voice of our feelings and respond from the voice of our spirit. We always have a choice in how we will respond to situations no matter how we are treated. We must learn to step over our hijacked emotions so we can make decisions that will benefit us. God is never afraid of our strong feelings.

Surround yourself with people who will speak truth, into your life (John 8:32). If we pursue people who will agree with what our feelings are telling us, we will remain in the rut we are in. All of us need truth spoken to us in love to help us choose correctly. Life and death are in the power of the tongue, (Prov. 18:21). As we read in the Psalms we see how real King David was with God. God wants us to be real about the battles we face. He does not want us to bring a sanitized version of our troubles to Him, but the reality of the battle.

A mentor is one who shares their experience & learning with another. A mentee is a person who is advised, trained or counselled by a mentor. Each of us must take the initiative to learn what we need to learn. As we pour into and receive from others, God pours into us. Be intentional to ask our teacher, Holy Spirit, for the answers you need first. Often we rely too much on people rather than Holy Spirit for counsel. As a mentee, posture yourself with a spirit of humility. Remember, a good attitude is more conducive to learning than a big aptitude!

People can share information with us, but understanding comes from God. As a mentor, model how to remain balanced through a foundation of God's Word. As a mentor, develop a healthy detachment from the mentee, empowering them to choose how fast they progress. Elijah had just seen the greatest victory of his life against Jezebel and more than 450 prophets. He found himself under a broom tree wanting to die. An angel came to him two times, saying get up and eat for the journey is long. He was ministered to by God through His angel, (1 Kings 19:5). Although Elijah had responded in fear of Jezebel, God met Elijah at his point of need and redirected him.

As God helped Elijah, we are to help others also. Cover a mentee's mistakes so they are not humiliated. In private, explain to them why what they did was not correct and explain a better way. Consider the words you use to convey the information as well as the attitude of your heart and the setting you speak to them in. People may respond to well intended coaching with a sense of rejection because of their own wounds. If love and acceptance of the person undergird the message, it is often accepted and received.

As a mentor, we can only pour out to others what we have received from God. We all need to listen to what God is speaking to us. Do not try to make a clone of yourself but rather allow them to learn from Holy Spirit. Encourage the mentee to become who God made them to be. God made each of us uniquely different as He loves uniqueness. Give them freedom to be themselves as they learn how the anointing and the gifts of Holy Spirit will operate through them. Encourage the mentee to operate within the guidelines of honour and respect so they will give Glory to God. Each of us must remember, God is the source of all wisdom to grow in the gift of prophecy.

As I developed through a mentorship program, I learned that Holy Spirit wants us to meditate on some questions as a method of giving us greater understanding. Encourage those learning to spend time actively listening to all God wants to tell them. Everyone hears differently and this skill of asking and listening must be cultivated and practiced.

There is a cost to walk as a disciple of Jesus Christ. "Then Jesus said to His disciples, whoever wants to be My disciple must deny themselves and take up their cross and follow Me" (Matt 16:24). Our own desires will fight us from following God any way they can. The devil will work through our flesh to get us moving away from God. We see an example of this in the life of Paul. "Paul and his companions traveled throughout the region of Phrygia and Galatia, having been kept by Holy Spirit from preaching the word in the province of Asia" (Acts 16:6). God gave Paul a dream of a man in Macedonia requesting Paul come to them and preach the gospel. "During the night Paul had a vision of a man of Macedonia standing and begging him, come over to Macedonia and help us" (Acts 16:9). Holy Spirit directed the movement of Paul as he preached the gospel. Holy Spirit is fulfilling the will of God through men and women on the earth even today. As Holy Spirit blocked Paul from going to places He did not want, He will do the same with us. As He directed Paul to a different location, He will do the same with us. Each of us will be faced with change in our lives to do what God tells us to do. What appears to be a set back is often a set up for a promotion in God's kingdom.

Speaking the truth in love in all situations is key. As humans we rationalize what we call little white lies. A lie is a lie no matter how we explain it. When we allow lies to exist in our lives, we allow the devil opportunity to hold us back. For example, the phone rings and it is a person you do not want to speak with. You say to the one who answered the phone, "tell them I am not home." When this is done, we have asked another to lie for us. We can twist the truth to avoid saying no to people or hurting their feelings. We must get to the place where we want the truth to be spoken in love more than anything else.

At the cross Jesus dealt with every issue of sin to set us free. There is no legal argument the accuser can make that can trump the legal authority of the blood of Christ. The price was paid. In God's eyes we are free.

We confess our sin to the Father, ask for forgiveness in Jesus name. Then say, "I declare the legal authority of the blood of Christ, breaking all power of the enemy, in Jesus name." When our Father completed the plan of salvation, He gave us this legal authority to defeat all arguments of the enemy. We believe what He said is true and receive through faith in what Jesus did for us. When we ask for forgiveness to be saved, we do not see anything change in the natural but believe what God said to be true. In the same way we believe in the legal authority of the blood of Christ to free us of any bondage.

We have received an "unrestricted" pass into God's presence, through the name of Jesus. "If you remain in me and my words remain in you, ask whatever you wish and it will be done for you" (John 15:7). As we obey Jesus out of love for Him, we will receive what we ask for in His name. Also, Jesus said, "And these signs will accompany those who believe: in my name they will drive out demons; they will speak in new tongues; they will pick up snakes with their hands; and when they drink deadly poison it will not hurt them at all; they will place their hands on sick people and they will get well" (Mark 16:17-18). We have been given authority to set others free from ways they are bound through the name of Jesus.

Jesus gave us the Lord's Supper to participate in regularly for our benefit. He said, "Do this in remembrance of Me" (1 Corinthians 11:23-26). We can participate in taking the Lord's Supper in a church gathering or take it as a few believers together. The instructions for the Lord's Supper are given in 1 Corinthians 11:23-30. A piece of bread or cracker represents the body of Jesus for the Lord's Supper. A cup of grape juice represents the blood of Christ shed for us. My wife and I will take the Lord's Supper at home when we feel to do so. One of us will thank Jesus for His Body that was broken for our healing. We will say, "Lord, you told us to celebrate what you did for us through this ordinance. We receive all you intended to give us through the breaking of your body for us in faith." Then we will break the bread or cracker and eat it. Then the other one of us will thank Jesus for His blood that was shed for the remission of all our sin. Then we will drink the grape juice. After the emblems are taken, we will spend a bit of time praising Jesus for all He did for us on the cross. We will say, "Lord we receive all you intended to give us through this ordinance by faith." There is no specified number of times we should celebrate this ordinance. It is my belief that we should celebrate it once per month as a guideline. We can receive healing through celebrating this ordinance in faith. I recommend that you begin celebrating this as part of your faith walk.

When Jesus ascended back to heaven, He sat down at the right hand of the Father as our High Priest. He intercedes for us, perfecting our prayers that go to the Father. We can trust that Jesus knows our heart's desires and He will ensure what we are asking for is communicated to thc Father. For years I battled a lie that if I did not ask for exactly what I wanted, I would not receive what I was asking for. God showed me how I was believing He would respond as people who let me down did. Since God is good all the time, we can trust in Jesus to communicate our desires to the Father even when we do not correctly communicate our desires to Him. Holy Spirit, who is our teacher, will help us to pray effective prayers to God.

Through this chapter we have looked at many choices we need to make to grow as a disciple. As we rely on God's grace while walking in humility, God's favour will rest upon us for the process.

Chapter 3

The Purposes of Tongues

Tongues is a prayer language we receive from God when we are baptized in Holy Spirit. This is a gift from the Father that we can use any time we choose. As we pray in tongues, we partner with what God wants to do in this world. Scripture states, "All of them were filled with Holy Spirit and began to speak in other tongues as the Spirit enabled them" (Acts 2:4). The following will look at the multiple functions, the gift of tongues fulfills, for a believer, walking in the gifts of the Spirit.

In Scripture we read that as one prays in tongues they converse with God in an unknown language. "For anyone who speaks in a tongue does not speak to people but to God. Indeed, no one understands them; they utter mysteries by the Spirit" (1 Corinthians 14:2). As we pray in tongues, we build up our faith. "But you dear friends by building yourself up in your most holy faith and praying in Holy Spirit, keep yourselves in God's love as you wait for the mercy of our Lord Jesus Christ to bring you to eternal life" (Jude 1:20-21). Holy Spirit helps us as we pray in tongues to pray the will of God by giving us utterance. "In the same way the Spirit helps us in our weakness. We do not know what to pray for but the Spirit Himself intercedes for us through wordless groans. And He who searches our hearts knows the mind of the Spirit, because the Spirit intercedes for God's people in accordance with the will of God" (Romans 8:26-27). This is an important point to recognize. None of us know the perfect will of God. We know things from reading His word and from revelation He has given us. As we submit to Holy Spirit and pray in tongues, He will give us utterance to pray the will of God for ourselves and others.

When we know what God wants and we ask for it we shall receive what we ask for. This is why praying in tongues is such a powerful aid for us. We have Holy Spirit who knows the will of God, enabling us to ask for what God wants to give us so that we can receive it. Through praying in tongues, God does for us what no person can do.

Holy Spirit builds strength into our spirit through us praying in tongues. The same supernatural power that raised Jesus from the dead is present when we pray in tongues. We can pray in tongues whenever, wherever and as often as we want to build ourselves up. Praying in tongues can be done out loud or silently in our mind. All we need to do is tap into the flow of the Spirit. According to how much time we will dedicate to praying in tongues, we shall be edified or built up.

It is important for us to understand that we must do the praying in tongues. Holy Spirit does not pray for us. In the same way that we speak out words in prayer to God, we need to speak out the words in the language of tongues. God said, my people perish from lack of knowledge. We are robbed of the benefits of praying in tongues through holding on to incorrect beliefs. For us to benefit, we need to decide if we will receive this gift from God and if we will operate in this gift.

As I prepare to pray in the spirit, I will say something like this to Holy Spirit. "Lord, thank you for giving me utterance to pray the will of God for myself and others. Thank you for enabling me to edify myself as I pray in tongues." Then, I will begin to pray in tongues. As I pray, I pay attention to what thoughts the Lord brings to my mind. Any information I feel Holy Spirit is highlighting, I will speak it out like this. "I thank you Father for blessing the people of Canada. Thank you for our government officials making good decisions that are benefiting all of the people in Canada." Then I will go back into tongues. As I dance between praying in tongues and my English language, God's will is being prayed.

As we set aside specific time to pray in tongues, we cooperate with Holy Spirit to do many things. This does not make sense to our natural mind, but to grow in the things of God, we must let God teach us His ways. We need to allow Jesus to challenge our theology with His truth. God wants us to succeed in doing what He has called us to do, but He needs our cooperation with His plan. If we continually look for things to be as we expect them to be, we will be disappointed. God does things His way, in His time. The life of a disciple is to follow Jesus through the leading of Holy Spirit, including praying in tongues. As we obey Him, we will receive additional tongues for intercession, praise, singing etc. Holy Spirit will increase our languages in tongues so we can fulfill the work He has for us to do.

In my life I began with one language in tongues. It seemed that each time I would pray in tongues this was the language I would hear. After several years of praying in tongues, one day I heard myself praying differently. As I listened to the words coming out of my mouth, I recognized they were different. Then it seemed I had two different languages that I prayed in. After several more years I detected another new language I was praying in. As I operate today, I find I have one language that operates as I give corporate words of prophecy, a different language that operates as I pray in tongues to edify myself and a third language that I pray for people in prayer ministry. That being said, we can grow from where we are to where God is calling us. Each of us is in control of how far we go with God. Will we purposefully dedicate the time to praying in tongues in order to grow? Will we sacrifice to receive what God wants to give us? The choice is ours. I encourage you to embrace and grow in this powerful gift God has given us.

In a corporate gathering, when tongues are spoken out, it is for unbelievers proving that God is real. "Tongues, then, are a sign, not for believers but for unbelievers; prophecy, however, is not for unbelievers but for believers" (1 Corinthians 14:22). Scripture tells us to not forbid speaking in tongues, "Therefore my brothers and sisters, be eager to prophesy and do not forbid speaking in tongues. But everything should be done in a fitting and orderly way" (1 Corinthians 14:39-40). Following this admonishment, we should pursue to flow with the church service or fellowship group we are in. Tongues and an interpretation are used by God to call someone to salvation, to rededicate their lives to Jesus, to change the direction they are going in their walk with Him and to confirm the message a speaker is to bring in a service.

Prayer is a conversation with God, bringing our needs, thanking and worshiping Him. Intercession is the conversation of one or more people bringing the circumstances of a person, a group or a nation before God. As we intercede in tongues Holy Spirit will bring distinct thoughts through our mind. We will have people's names and details go through our mind as we pray. We intercede for these people asking for those things that are going through our mind.

Intercession for people that God places on our hearts takes time and focus. As one is moved to intercede for people they may pray for a few minutes to a few months. If we persist in intercession, the strategy of the evil one is destroyed. We partner with God, through The Holy Spirit to bless and touch other people through our prayers.

As we are called to intercede for others, we will contend with evil forces on behalf of other people. This intercession can push back the spiritual forces to enable the person we are interceding for to receive what they need from the Lord and hopefully respond to His prompting. Additionally, through praying in tongues, we can pray for situations in advance, preventing them from occurring.

Another way Holy Spirit utilizes tongues is seen on the Day of Pentecost, (Acts 2). As Holy Spirit came upon the disciples as tongues of fire and they began to speak in other tongues. As the disciples spoke aloud in tongues the spirit enabled those present to hear what was said in their own language. There was a large number of people present from every nation speaking many different languages. A crowd of these people came together in bewilderment because each one heard their own language being spoken as the disciples spoke in other tongues. They heard the disciples declaring the wonders of God in their own language. Some reacted by claiming the disciples were drunk as there was not a logical explanation for what had just occurred. Through speaking in tongues, God displays He is real and at work in the lives of people.

In Scripture we read that we edify ourselves as we pray in tongues. What does this mean, to edify ourselves? The definition of edifying is to instruct or to improve someone morally or intellectually. Synonyms are to educate, teach, train, guide, enlighten. It is my belief that as we pray in tongues, we allow Holy Spirit to strengthen us in our understanding of truth, to enlighten us to truth we have not understood and to position ourselves to be taught greater truths. In yielding to Holy Spirit, we are humbling ourselves and admitting we need Him to speak greater truth and guidance into our lives.

As we pray in tongues, our prayers bypass our mind. As our mind is not involved in prayer, we will not get into unbelief and therefore will see our prayers in tongues answered.

Through the operation of tongues and interpretation of those tongues, we can receive answers to the many questions we have. God said, "Ask and it will be given to you, seek and you will find, knock and the door will be opened to you. For everyone who asks receives" (Matthew 7:7-8). The answers will come for questions we have asked God and man. As we go through our day, we need to include praying in tongues. Some of the questions we ask will be answered through the interpretation of those tongues. When the interpretation comes, our spirit will witness to us that the interpretation is from Holy Spirit. The interpretation will come in God's timing, we cannot force it. It may not come immediately after we pray in tongues, but minutes or weeks after praying in tongues. The interpretation can come through ourselves, another person, a song, a sign, a newspaper, or any form of communication. Holy Spirit is not limited in how He can speak to us. We need to learn to keep our radar up so that we will hear from Him whenever and however He speaks to us. As I am writing this book, I regularly pray in tongues. At different times I would have distinct thoughts come to mind that I knew were for the book. I learned to carry a small notepad with me to capture those thoughts as they came.

We have learned that tongues is a gift from God that is utilized in the life of believers. We see that God uses this gift in different ways to benefit us and others as we choose to operate in it.

Chapter 4

Corporate Prophecy

In this chapter we will look into one of the ways prophecy operates to bring encouragement, confirmation and direction to those in the body of believers. We will see that prophecy can speak to a corporate body and individuals at the same time, through the same word.

Wherever you have a number of believers present in an environment of faith, corporate prophecy may occur regardless of the venue. Corporate prophecy happens as the Spirit of God moves on the heart of a believer to prophesy. Prophecy in this case is to bring direction, confirmation and revelation to the body of believers as well as individuals.

As a person is moved upon by Holy Spirit to prophesy, there can be some physical manifestations experienced. These can feel like a quiet stirring, our heart racing, upset stomach, increased pulse, sweating, an urgency or a feeling of peace. One can sense a repeating of a few words over and over, a similar theme or thought going through their mind. These experiences will vary from one person to another. It has been my experience that one may experience greater manifestations as they prepare to give a corporate word of prophecy than an individual word of prophecy. We must learn to control our body as Holy Spirit comes on us to speak a word of prophecy.

Scripture tells us, "For you can all prophesy in turn so that everyone may be instructed and encouraged" (1 Corinthians 14:31). So, if all can prophesy, why is it that all do not prophesy? First, we must believe what God said in the Bible about prophecy, that the gift of prophecy is still alive and continues to operate through born again believers today. We must be willing to let go of our understanding and current experience to embrace what God's Word tells us. We need to be willing to step out in faith speaking what Holy Spirit communicates to us. We must stop allowing our intellect to claim that what Holy Spirit shows us makes no sense.

Prophecy originates with God. In its simplest form God speaks, we listen. Then, we repeat what we heard God tell us to another person or group. A prophetic word is a spontaneous, divinely given understanding or foreknowledge about a person or an event. It can range from a single word to a number of sentences.

Corporate prophecy speaks to the church as a whole. This word can come in tongues with an interpretation or as a word of prophecy in the language of the people. A corporate word can speak to individuals at the same time it speaks to the body as a whole. These words bring answers to questions and direction to the body of Christ to confirm what God has been speaking to them. The apostle Paul has given us guidelines for the operation of prophecy in 1 Corinthians 12-14. The instruction is to eagerly desire gifts of the spirit, especially prophecy which applies to all people in a church service as a body of believers.

If during a service, you feel Holy Spirit stirring a word of prophecy in you, settle yourself to listen to what He is speaking to you. When you feel you have received what He has spoken, look for an opportunity to speak out the word of prophecy loud enough for all to hear. Speak the word of prophecy in the language of the people or tongues as you feel led by God.

As you are part of a church service and a word of prophecy is spoken out, listen closely to what is spoken. A corporate word of prophecy can apply to the corporate gathering as well as individuals in the meeting. If the word could apply to you, test it to see if it aligns with God's word and character. When you believe the word is from God tell Him you receive this from Him. Thank Him for the word. Believe Him to bring it into your life.

In order for the church to be edified a word spoken in tongues must be interpreted into the language of the people. If a person is present where a word is spoken out in tongues, they should ask Holy Spirit for an interpretation. When they receive the interpretation, they should look for an opportunity to speak this out. If others have interpreted, ask Holy Spirit if He wants additional interpretations spoken. Do not condemn yourself if you miss it, pursue to learn from the Lord. If there is no one who can interpret a word in tongues, the person who would speak in tongues should remain quiet, (1 Corinthians 14:28).

On other occasions, Holy Spirit will come upon a person to speak out in tongues. Although this is an unknown language to the speaker, some present will hear what is said in their own language. As the person hears what is spoken in their own language, they are encouraged that God is among them. This occurred on the Day of Pentecost where the people heard in their own language what was spoken in tongues.

As two or three prophets speak, their words should be weighed to determine what God is speaking to the body of Christ. Scripture tells us the spirit of a prophet is subject to the prophet. A person bringing a word of prophecy may feel they must give the word now which is common, but a person can hold on to a word for a few minutes to a few years before they release it. God is growing us to be able to receive greater words of revelation from His heart for His church. Although we will make mistakes, as we allow God to teach us, we will receive greater understanding on how to do things correctly.

As we begin receiving prophetic words from God, we may feel an overwhelming sense that we must speak it out immediately. This happens as there is a stirring of the Spirit of God in us. We can be overcome with His presence when we are not familiar with it. There is a correct time for releasing both corporate and individual words. Wait while pursuing confirmation from Holy Spirit for when to speak. Scripture tells us, "The spirits of prophets are subject to the control of prophets" (1 Corinthians 14:32). This confirms that we can receive a word from God, hold on to that word and release it at a later time.

We could receive a word in a service that does not fit with the flow of that service. The word we received could be for a different time in the future or for an individual. We may feel we have a word for a person, but the circumstances will not give us an opportunity to speak that word. Do not berate yourself. We cannot deliver a word if we do not have an opportunity to do so.

Our immediate action should be to ask the Lord about this. As we allow Him opportunity, He can show us if we have misunderstood what the word was for. It is important to remember we can make mistakes in hearing from God. It is my practice when I receive a word from the Lord but have no opportunity to speak it, to ask God about it. I will ask Him to correct me if I have misunderstood the meaning of the word. When a word of prophecy comes, it could be for a corporate setting, an individual, something for me to pray about or it could simply be God making me aware of what is occurring in the spirit realm. In cases such as these, I will thank God for the word.

When visiting a different church where prophecy could flow, ask someone in charge if they are open to prophetic words in tongues or in the language of the people. Ask what their protocol is to be followed to honour that house. Be proactive to learn this so you can be a blessing to those you are visiting. God is a God of order. We need to learn how to bring forth words in a way that will honour people. Words of prophecy can also be written out and given to the leaders for them to test and speak out as they feel appropriate. Special holiday services, miracle meetings, special teaching services, may not be the correct time or place to give words of prophecy. As we place ourselves in different environments, we will learn how Holy Spirit responds in different settings.

We learn as we step out in obedience, even when we make mistakes. As we become more experienced in bringing words of prophecy, the process becomes easier.

Chapter 5

Individual Prophecy

In the previous chapter we learned about prophecy operating in a corporate setting. This chapter will look at prophecy spoken to individuals and how it edifies people of all walks of life.

Individual prophecy occurs when one person receives a word from God for another person, then speaks that word to them. When we receive a word of prophecy for an individual, we need to be mindful of how that word is delivered. We should be aware that not all people are familiar with words of prophecy. Ask the person if they would like to receive the word. Explain that a word of prophecy is a personal word from God, expressing His hearts desire for them. If they say no, honour their decision and say no more. If they say yes, speak the word as you understand Holy Spirit has shown you.

Prophetic words can encourage, challenge, and correct us. Prophetic words do not bring condemnation, blame or inflict guilt upon a person. We should receive words that correct us, asking God for help to understand where we need to change. We should not accept any word that brings condemnation, as this is not from God.

When you are approached by someone that tells you they have a prophetic word for you, do not be alarmed. God speaks through people to bring encouragement, exhortation and comfort to His children. Ask to record the word with your phone as they speak it. Listen closely to what the person speaks. Once the word is spoken, responsibility for that word belongs to the recipient. A recorded word can be played over many times to give a clearer understanding.

Words of prophecy will contain words and images the recipient will relate to, with the flavour of the person speaking the word. Understanding and unpacking a prophetic word is a process. Ask Holy Spirit for wisdom to understand the word and how to apply the word to your life.

When I receive a word from the Lord, I will record it when possible so I can review it later. After I have received the word, I will speak with God about the word asking for wisdom to comprehend what He meant. I will thank God for the word like this; "Father, thank you for the word you spoke to me through your servant. I receive this word from You, believing you will bring it into my life. Show me my part in this word coming into reality."

In situations where I have received a word that I thought was not correct, I would put it aside, asking Holy Spirit to show me if any part of this word was correct. In this I remain open to what God has for me that may not yet be clear.

Someone new to receiving words of prophecy can be left wondering what these words mean. Is this word literal? How long does this take to happen? What do I have to do? Many questions will run through a person's mind as they work to unpack the prophetic word. Be honest as you explain the way a word of prophecy comes into our lives. It is ok to admit you do not understand aspects of this. Encourage them to speak with God about these aspects.

Words, numbers and symbols have general meanings to us as people. These same words can have a different meaning to God. To interpret a word of prophecy one must ask Holy Spirit for help. It is important to remember; God is speaking to a person about a matter He wants to communicate. Holy Spirit will give the interpretation of what was said and how it applies to the person's life. He may do this independently or use people or resources to bring thoughts to our mind.

We cannot interpret if we cannot hear the voice of Holy Spirit. Another person may tell you what they think the meaning is yet miss what God meant. It is God that spoke the prophetic word to us. It is essential that Holy Spirit is involved to interpret that word. God has shown me that as I meditate on the word, He will bring the meaning. Some interpretations will be easy and come quickly, others will take time as we wait for Holy Spirit to reveal the meaning.

Words can have different meanings to God than they do to us. We need to hear from God as to what He meant for us to understand. Some words may not appear relevant initially, but meditating on them will bring understanding of their meaning.

We previously read the guidelines for prophecy in 1 Corinthians 12 - 14. In these guidelines Paul speaks of us operating in love. For the delivery of personal words of prophecy, I will suggest some guidelines to follow for a positive interaction with others as a word of prophecy is given.

Introduce yourself to the person

Tell them you believe you have a word of prophecy from the Lord for them

Ask the person if they would like to receive this word

If they say no, respect them and say no more.

If they say yes, ask them if they wish to record the word on their phone

Speak the word in a place where the one receiving can clearly hear what is said

Be respectful when giving a word to one of opposite sex

When the word is given, ask them if the word resonated with them and if God had been speaking to them about this previously? What words are significant to you? Encourage the person to talk about the word with Holy Spirit asking for wisdom to comprehend what He is telling them.

If the person reacts to the word of prophecy and you believe it was from God, apologize for any way you offended them. We are not above making mistakes. If we will humble ourselves in a case like this, we give Holy Spirit opportunity to work on the person's heart to receive the word spoken. Remember, "We know in part and we prophesy in part" (1 Corinthians 13:9).

There are two kinds of words of prophecy we see with God. The first is a word that comes from Him that He will do something no matter what. An example is where Jesus calls Lazarus to come out of the grave. Lazarus was dead four days so he was not able to respond to the word of God with any action of faith. Jesus spoke to Lazarus in a loud voice, "Lazarus come out" (John 11:43). The spoken word brought life back to Lazarus dead body and he walked out of the grave.

The second kind of prophetic word is one where the recipient plays a part in it coming to pass. An example is where a word is spoken either corporately or individually, that will break the chains for the person the word is intended for. This is seen where Jesus spoke to the centurion who came to Him about his ill servant. Jesus spoke "Go! Let it be done, just as you believed it would" (Matthew 8:5-13). As the centurion responded to the spoken word in faith, the power of the spoken word healed the servant. We can also observe the power of the spoken word today as a word of knowledge is spoken over a person and they are healed from an ailment. The ailment is healed by the spoken word. A more significant illustration is a word of knowledge that God is healing a part of a person's body at a miracle service. As the person responds to the word of knowledge in faith, their body is healed.

Scripture says, "You do not have because you do not ask God" (James 4:2). We need to recognize our responsibility and ask God for help to understand what our response is to be to His word. "Ask and it will be given to you, seek and you will find, knock and the door will be opened to you. For everyone who asks receives, the one who seeks finds and to the one who knocks the door will be opened" (Matthew 7:7-8). We need to agree with what God has said. As an act of faith, speak out loud, "Lord I receive this word from you." Be obedient, doing what God shows you to do, as an act of faith.

Our disobedience can cause God to change His mind and not give us what was spoken in a prophetic word. Saul was anointed King (1 Sam. 10:1), but he was disobedient. Saul did not wait for Samuel the prophet to offer the sacrifice but decided to offer the sacrifice himself because Samuel the prophet seemed to be arriving late. "You have done a foolish thing, Samuel said. You have not kept the command the Lord God gave you" (1 Sam. 13:13). Disobedience cost Saul the position of being King. A prophetic word is God expressing His heart's desire to us, not a guarantee. God is no respecter of persons; He wants each of us to receive. A good response to a prophetic word is to speak about it to God using words such as:

Lord, I believe you have spoken to me through your servant. I receive what you have spoken to me. Give me wisdom to comprehend what you are telling me. Show me my part to see this word become reality in my life. I thank you in Jesus name.

As God calls us to respond to His word to us, some things or prophetic acts will challenge us to the point of appearing to be ridiculous. Let us look back to the House of Judah coming up against the walls of Jericho. God told them to do things that were prophetic acts: to walk around the walls of the city one time each day for 6 days. Put worshipers at the front of the processional, praising Him as they did this. On the seventh day walk around the city walls seven times. When this is done sound a long blast on the trumpets and have the whole army give a loud shout, (Joshua 6:5). As the people did what God said to do, He caused the walls around the city to collapse.

A New Testament example of a prophetic act is the following. "After we had been there a number of days, a prophet named Agabus came down from Judea. Coming over to us, he took Paul's belt, tied his own hands and feet with it and said, Holy Spirit says, in this way the Jewish leaders in Jerusalem will bind the owner of this belt and will hand them over to the Gentiles" (Acts 21:10-11). God had Agabus tie his hands with Paul's belt as He spoke the word to emphasize the message from God.

To anyone who needs to understand first, doing what God asks them to do could seem utterly ridiculous! Holy Spirit directs us in what to do and how to do it. Great power from God is released as people step out in faith following the direction of Holy Spirit as they do what they have been asked to do. Through obedience to God, great freedom can be brought to a person, group of people or a region.

In the New Testament we see Philip as part of the biggest move of God that was ever seen in Jerusalem. In the midst of God moving in Jerusalem, Holy Spirit told Philip to go over to Samaria. Humanly speaking this did not make sense. However, as Philip obeyed Holy Spirit, a huge revival broke out. It was so big that they asked Peter and John to come down and help out. When we are obedient to Holy Spirit, we will see God move in amazing ways even though it does not make sense to our understanding.

One major focus of a prophet's life is to pray for the needs of others as prompted by God. This can be called prophetic intercession. In prophetic intercession, Holy Spirit moves on the hearts of people to pray prayers beyond their knowledge and often using the gift of tongues. The prayers bubble up and are spoken out, empowered by Holy Spirit. The Greek word for this is Naba, meaning to bubble up. A person can pray for another person anywhere in the world by following the leading of Holy Spirit. Through praying in tongues, we can speak the will of God into the atmosphere as Holy Spirit gives us utterance. What is spoken in tongues can be interpreted by another person at another place and time to give encouragement, direction or confirmation to another.

Jesus spoke to Ananias asking him to go pray for Paul that he could receive his sight back, (Acts 9:10-17). The Lord called Ananias in a vision. Ananias went to Paul, laid his hands on him and prayed that he would receive his sight and be filled with Holy Spirit. The result was that Paul received his sight and the baptism of Holy Spirit. As we are obedient to do what God tells us to do, He will perform great miracles.

Chapter 6

Priorities of Your Day

In previous chapters we have looked at different ways words of prophecy are delivered and received. In this chapter we will look at what things we give time to and how this affects our walk with God and operating in the gift of prophecy.

To be effective for God we must begin our day by aligning ourselves with God. This requires that we order our day with the correct priorities. We must decide what we are going to do and what we are not. "But seek first His kingdom and His righteousness and all these things will be given to you as well" (Matthew 6:33). We are told by Jesus that if we place our priority in the correct place, seeking the Father first, we shall receive all we need in our day.

I will share a familiar analogy with you. Our day is symbolized by a 5-gallon pail. Our priorities are symbolized from smallest using sand to largest using large rocks. If we allow small priorities represented by sand to be placed in our pail first, we will not get the large rocks, or big priorities into our day. The small priorities we have allowed, have taken the place of the large priority. As wise servants, we should structure our day by placing big priorities in our day first. The big priorities in our day begin with pursuing the Father and giving Him time at the beginning of our day. As we begin this way, the small priorities will flow into our day around the larger priorities. This requires intentional action on our part. If we are passive, other people will decide our priorities for us. Examples are phone calls, a knock at the door, a message from Facebook, where someone needs you to help them now. By spending time with God first, we will be better positioned to assist people we interact with in our day. We must learn to say no to good things in order to say yes to God.

We say we love God and want to please Him. Do we give Him the right to change our plans? As prophetic people we speak words over others from the heart of God. These words of prophecy flow through us, out of our relationship with God. The closer our walk is, the more clearly we shall hear from Him, so we must learn to treasure the time we have together. His desire is that we learn His ways as we allow Holy Spirit to teach and guide us.

As Moses said to God, teach me your ways, we would be wise to ask the same thing. As we are in an intimate relationship with God, it would make sense that we treat our relationship with Him better than we treat our best friend. He longs for us to welcome Him into every part of our lives. As we do this, we honour Him. We can be with God yet be distant from Him. We can be in the same place as Him but not be receiving all He wants us to give us. We can deeply hurt Holy Spirit by inconsiderate and insincere behaviour.

Justifying inconsiderate behaviour leads us into error. If you blow it or get distracted, go to God asking for forgiveness. Own your mistakes by admitting them to God. He will quickly forgive you. We walk in grace, get back on track and move on. God wants relationship because we are His children. Go through your day giving Him thanks in all circumstances.

Our day needs to begin with us displaying a grateful heart. As I wake, I begin my day with speaking to God, "Good morning Holy Spirit." I thank Him for the day He has given me and invite Him into it. Aligning ourselves with God first thing in our day is an important step to being a conduit for Him. I have established a priority where I read God's Word then meditate on what I read. Mornings may not be a desirable time for you, but each of us needs to be intentional welcoming God into our day. A healthy hunger for intimacy with God will drive us to incorporate healthy spiritual disciplines into our life. Take ownership of your choices by pushing things out of your day to give God His rightful place.

The direction of our day can be changed by us deciding to do something different. In order to move to deeper intimacy, we must learn what pleases God. We often hear God's voice and sense His direction in quiet and stillness. Whether it is in quiet or in the background of soft music, each of us needs to discover how we best hear from God.

We can hear about God the Father, God the Son and God Holy Spirit, but through spending time with Him we discover who He is. We cultivate relationship through reading God's Word, speaking to and hearing from Him. As we do this, we experience more of His presence. The more of His presence we experience the more we learn about who He is.

"Do not conform to the pattern of this world, but be transformed by the renewing of your mind. Then you will be able to test and approve what God's will is, His good, pleasing and perfect will" (Romans 12:2). As we incorporate reading and meditating on God's Word in our day, we will see our mind being transformed. As our mind is transformed, we will be able to determine His will for us. This is why I feel this practice needs to be at the beginning of our day. I give God thanks for who He is and all the ways He has blessed our family. Also, I come into agreement with what God has said about our family and declare that out loud.

We live in a time of grace with no formula. Each of us needs to discover how to interact with God in ways that will take us into deeper intimacy with Him. The secret place is a place where close friends gather to share intimate time together. This secret place is kept between the meeting parties as a secret. Our Father desires that we discover the secret place with Him.

To visit is to go with the intention of leaving. To dwell is to go with the intention of remaining there. The secret place can be symbolized by pictures, journaling, soaking, nature, reading His word and worshiping to name a few ways. Our Father desires that we commune with Him in the secret place. To commune is where two people are in a position, similar to being in bed together where nothing lies between them. He wants us to feel safe to discuss any issues in our heart. We come to know God's heart through reading His word, understanding His character, asking Him questions and listening to him speak. Holding on to false beliefs can hold us back from discovering the secret place. He wants us to be free to ask Him any questions as part of our learning. By asking open-ended questions, we are open to receive His answer even when it is different than we want. A few examples of open-ended questions are; "Father, how do you see me as your child?", "Father, describe how you see me as a tree planted beside the streams of life.", "Father, what would you wish to tell me today?" It is best to ask questions that are not answered by yes or no. The goal is to hear what the Father wants to speak from His heart to yours.

When we dwell with God, we can receive what we need easily. When we only visit God occasionally, we feel we must beg Him for what we need. God wants us to walk through our day in continual fellowship with Him. He desires that we make Him part of our family relationships, our home, our work, our church life, our time, our money, our resources etc. As we dwell in the secret place, we allow God to permeate our life with His presence. He wants us to discuss everything with Him, the good and the bad, giving thanks in all circumstances. Since we speak to God about matters, we do not panic when a challenge comes. We discuss the situation with God, believe He hears us and will help us.

Fear prevents us from opening up parts of our life to God. What will He think of me if I tell Him I struggle with this problem? Will He discipline me or reject me like other people did? God knows everything about us already, nothing in our lives will surprise Him. Even though Jesus knows our struggles and that we try to hide parts of our life from Him, He still loves us. He stands with arms wide open receiving us even in the midst of our struggles. As we grow in deeper relationship with Jesus, He will begin to share secrets from His heart for only us to know.

We learn in this world that some information is sensitive so we are careful not to share it with just anyone. Sensitive information is selectively shared to protect someone from being hurt. What we need to understand is that Jesus entrusts us with secrets from His heart that are very sensitive to Him. We need to treat what Jesus reveals to us with sensitivity and respect. Recognize the honour He gives us in sharing these treasures with us. Jesus wants us to know Him as a friend while always reverencing Him as Lord of all. Ask Him to help you envision the secret place, what this place looks like, smells like and feels like. Ask Him for help to share secrets with Him that you would tell no other.

Many of us have not been able to find a secret place in this world or a person we could share our secrets with where we felt safe. As a result we may discount truths about Jesus through believing lies about Him. This is one way the devil steals from us. The Lord has revealed this secret place to us for our benefit. He is blessed as we learn of this place and begin to interact with Him through our day. We are the ones who are blessed the most through this interaction. An example of a secret place I go with Jesus is when I am home alone, to turn off all devices and speak with Him about what is on my heart. I will share my hopes and dreams with Him. As I do this, I will ask Him, Lord what is on your heart today that you would want to share with me? In discussion I will speak to Jesus of things I would not readily share with others. This would include speaking to Him about family members and those close to me. Also, I would look for clarity on the direction I feel He is giving me so that I can be more fully aligned with Him. My discussion will also include struggles I have with myself and others. A large part of our time together is me listening to what He wants to tell me. I treasure what Jesus speaks to me as I recognize it is important to Him. As we are intentional to begin this process, we will see our times of intimacy grow.

God speaks to us as we read His word. Holy Spirit will often cause words in a passage to jump off the page bringing them to our attention. Through regular reading of God's Word, we strengthen our understanding of God's ways. Throughout the Bible are promises God has made to us as His children. As we agree with these assurances and declare them over our lives, we speak powerful words. For example, Scripture tells us to bring all our cares and concerns to God with thanksgiving. As we bring these concerns to God, we give Him thanks for bringing the answers we need.

As we worship God, we set ourselves in a place to receive. As we freely give our worship to Him, He will communicate with us, touching our lives as we have need. As you go though your day, include God in every part of what you do. It is important to remember that God communicates differently than we as humans do. Do not discount the power of an encounter with Him because it was different than you expect. As we ask God for needs to be met, we must also be deliberate to thank Him for meeting those needs. Through thanking Him for honouring our prayer requests in advance, we display our faith in Him.

We must believe the Word of God as written in the Bible is truth. We do not need to understand it all, but we do need to believe it is the Word of God. God gave man a free will to choose. We can choose to walk to God and we can choose to walk away from God. We can choose the ways of God or the ways of this world. We need to understand what road we are on as we live our lives. "Enter through the narrow gate. For wide is the gate and broad is the road that leads to destruction and many enter through it. But small is the gate and narrow the road that leads to life and only a few find it" (Matthew 7:13-14). There is a way that appears to be right, but in the end it leads to death, (Proverbs 14:12). We require wisdom for all the decisions we make to keep us aligned with the goal God has for us.

"When I was a child, I talked like a child, I thought like a child, I reasoned like a child. When I became a man, I put the ways of childhood behind me" (1 Corinthians 13:11). As Scripture speaks of us maturing into adulthood, we put childish things behind us. God wants us to mature in all parts of our being, especially our interaction with Him. This requires that we replace incorrect beliefs about God with truth.

Being present and participating with the body of believers is important for us to succeed in our walk with God. We need encouragement, support, direction and counsel from fellow believers to stay the course. God is our source, yet He uses people to help us on the journey. Trying to do it alone is not God's best plan for our lives.

For us to receive from God we must learn the ways of God. We do this through reading His word and interacting with Him. Through the study of how God operated in the past, we can learn His ways. God is multidimensional, He is timeless, not bound by restraints in any way. We are bound by the limits of our body and mind in our existence on earth. Therefore, God's Word and other believers both contribute to keeping us focused on truth and its expression.

As previously stated, we receive from God as He speaks through His word, that still small voice, impressions, visions, dreams, nature and prophetically through other people. We receive from God as we attend Sunday service, as we interact with others. We receive by reading His word, sitting in His presence, conversing with Him. We receive as we pray in tongues. We receive as we intentionally place ourselves in His presence. An important key to receiving from God is learning to push back the demands of this world to hear from Him. We need to believe He hears us, cares for us and will give us what we need.

The life of a prophet is built upon an intimate relationship with God. Prayer is communication between us and God. Through prayer we bring our cares, concerns, our praise and worship before the Father. Prophetic people need to live in active prayer where there is continual speaking to and listening to God. Each of us needs God to teach us what is correct so we can fully receive from Him. I encourage you to pray the following prayer asking our Father to teach you what you do not know:

Father, teach me how to pray correctly according to Your word. Show me what your word tells me about prayer and who I am as a child of God so that I can see my prayers answered. I ask in Jesus name.

Many people get involved in ministry work allowing good ideas from others to determine their decisions. We allow people to become so important to us that we listen to them more than God. We allow the words of man to set our direction rather than God. Sometimes we do not take the time to ask God if the idea we have been given is from Him. The result is we get involved doing great things with no thought that we could be going in a different direction than God wants.

Through this chapter we have looked at who determines the priorities of our day. For any of us to walk as a prophet, we must determine what will get our time as we follow God through our day.

Chapter 7

Blossoming on the Journey

To blossom on the journey of becoming a prophet, it is essential to guard our heart. "Above all else, guard your heart, for everything you do flows from it" (Proverbs 4:23). As a man thinks, so is he, (Proverbs 23:7). The thoughts we allow to remain in our mind determine the direction of our lives.

Our first step is to become aware that a battle is occurring in our mind. Once we are aware, how do we battle against these attacks on our mind? "Do not conform to the pattern of this world, but be transformed by the renewing of your mind. Then you will be able to test and approve what God's will is – His good, pleasing and perfect will" (Romans 12:2). Our mind is renewed as we regularly read and meditate on the word of God.

Scripture provides us a recipe to follow and a guide of what to think on. "Finally brothers and sisters, whatever is true, whatever is noble, whatever is right, whatever is pure, whatever is lovely, whatever is admirable – if anything is excellent or praiseworthy, think about such things" (Philippians 4:8). We are instructed to focus on what is true, noble, right, etc. This means we can choose to change the focus of our mind to something positive.

As we go through our day, we need to be aware of our thoughts, assess our attitudes about people, situations and events. Through study of the word of God and listening to wise counsel, we can learn to detect the roots of deception in our mind.

God will help us recognize untruths, to remove and replace them with truth. However, this requires we do the heart work to bring change from the wounds of our past. This heart work, this inner healing, this renewing of our mind is necessary in order to walk in freedom and truth. Others can assist us doing this work, but no other person can do the work for us. Each of us must be willing to participate in doing the heart work to get free.

Often, we interpret comments through the filter of our past hurts. By arresting these thoughts and exposing our misbeliefs we stop the poisoning of our mind. As thoughts come into our mind, we determine which ones remain and which ones must leave. It is common to have repetitive negative thoughts come into our mind as the enemy bombards us in our areas of weakness.

The battle in our mind against negative thoughts is multi dimensional. Many voices are speaking to us in the flow of our mind at any given time. What we believe, both as truth and as lies, begin when we are very young. So, we can come to believe lies through agreement with things said by authority figures, family and culture. The enemy is constantly assaulting the truth of who we really are. To walk victoriously in our thinking, we need to renew our mind in truth, recognizing this is a process.

The process consists of overcoming lies we believe from authority figures, learning to rebuke the demonic and renew our mind with truth through spending time in God's presence and His word. For additional information I suggest you read the book, 'Battlefield of the Mind', winning the battle in your mind, by Joyce Meyer. Joyce gives a comprehensive approach to recognizing negative thoughts and how to stop them from controlling you.

Twenty-five years ago, I asked God to teach me to pray in an effort to understand Him more. As we ask, God will tell us things that will take time to fully understand. At the time I expected Him to give me some big complicated prayer to pray that would make me look important. Instead, the Lord said, "Ask me to remove the lies from your thinking and replace them with truth." I pondered on what He said to me. Two days later Holy Spirit said, "Steve, I want to show you something." Holy Spirit asked, "What do you see?" In my mind's eye I saw what looked like a piece of cooked bacon on its side, so I said, "I see a piece of bacon on its side." Holy Spirit said, "That is correct."

Then I saw the image turn so I saw it from the top. Again, Holy Spirit asked me, "What do you see?" I said, "I see a piece of steak surrounded by a piece of bacon." The Lord said, "That is correct. It is the same for a lie surrounded by truth. If we do not look at things from the right perspective, a lie will not be detected. Like the steak, when it is surrounded by the bacon, it cannot be seen from the side view, a lie surrounded by truth can only be seen from a certain point of view. The enemy will hide lies in your belief system that will affect your decisions and yet, they will appear to be truth. You need Me to remove these lies or they will continue to affect your decisions."

Tell God you come out of agreement with any lies of the enemy and into agreement with what He said. Ask Him to reveal and remove any lies that are holding you back. Changing the course of our life can be as simple as changing the thoughts we entertain and words we speak.

In the chart below are a few examples of a lie we believe about our self and what God's Word says about us.

My thought	**What does God's Word say**
I can do nothing right	I can do all this through Him who gives me strength (Phil 4:13)
I am a weak person	My grace is sufficient for you, for my power is made perfect in weakness (2 Cor. 12:9)
I am alone	Never will I leave you, never will I forsake you, (Hebrews 13:5)
I am hopeless	In His great mercy He has given us new birth into a living hope (1 Peter 1:3)

God said my people perish from lack of knowledge. As we cooperate with Holy Spirit, He will lead us into a different way of thinking. An example of wisdom in the natural is applying these principles; the use of medication, counselling, deliverance, inner healing or other forms of assistance for a season. Utilize the expertise of a physician, eat healthy, balanced meals at regular times. Ensure you get enough sleep and remove yourself from sources of unnecessary stress. Through addressing areas of our life that are out of balance in the natural, we move a step closer to having a healthier heart and mind. It may be necessary to set up healthy boundaries from others who would hinder your progress. We need to be willing to change many things to successfully get out from under the lies we have believed.

Through fasting we subdue the desires of our flesh to hear God more clearly. Holy Spirit may prompt us to fast for a specific cause or purpose. This may be to intercede for others, to pursue answers for our self or to grow in intimacy with God. To walk in the prophetic, we must be led by our spirit. If we are controlled by our soul (mind, will and emotions) or our life, we will not be strong spiritually. Fasting is a practice that requires one to deny themselves of food, drink or activities for a period of time in order to grow closer to God. As we consecrate ourselves through fasting, we position ourselves to hear more clearly from God. It is my belief that fasting should not become a religious ritual, but be done as led by the Spirit of God.

What is character and how is this developed in us? Character is doing what is right and correct no matter if someone is watching or not. It consists of living our lives following the guidelines God has given us in His word. Character is displayed in what we do and what we do not do, in good times and in bad, as a person of character responds to people and circumstances, according to God's word. In Romans 12, we see examples of how character is displayed in a person's life.

It is my understanding that character is formed through adversity God takes us through. This is the place where Holy Spirit removes those parts of our character that resist doing what God wants. God begins by teaching us that we work for Him, He does not work for us. He will even insult our intelligence to get our attention, so we can learn what He has to teach us. In this process, God addresses those areas of our life that hinder His working through us.

As we receive the gift of prophecy from Holy Spirit, we must learn to operate in this gift. There are similarities between operating in the gifts of the spirit and operating in our natural life. Responsibility for our growth resides with us. We need to dedicate time with Holy Spirit to learn what we need to learn. Our growth is determined by our willingness to give Holy Spirit our full attention and apply what He teaches us.

We can receive anointing from Holy Spirit yet lack wisdom to operate in this. It is necessary to ask God for wisdom to operate in the gift of prophecy. Each of us needs to learn how to operate in a supernatural gift to be a blessing to others in this world.

Attending training opportunities and getting networked with others who can help us grow in prophecy will benefit us. Most importantly is investing time developing our relationship with Holy Spirit. As our teacher here on earth, Holy Spirit knows what we need to become who we are called to be by God. As we give Holy Spirit permission to teach us, He will connect us with people and resources to develop us.

Many prophets are misunderstood, abused and labeled. Some in leadership positions do not understand the gift of prophecy, so they reject it or attack the one speaking it. It is important to walk in the gift of prophecy in unity with the Pastor.

To walk as a true humble servant, we need to want unity of the Spirit above all else. There will be times when the prophet and the pastor will strongly differ. Since God created both offices, we must put ego aside, pursuing what God wants in unity. Some prophets do not want to operate under authority. This behaviour can cause a rift between them and church leadership.

Some are thrust into prophecy with little notice. In a service, Holy Spirit can come on a person and they blurt out a word in tongues. If the behaviour seems to interrupt the flow of the service, the person could be reprimanded. It is important for us to learn how to deliver a word of prophecy honouring the church we attend so it can be received. We need to forgive those who correct us without understanding what really occurred. As God develops us, He will stretch us in ways that we are not comfortable.

Holy Spirit wants control over the tongue of any believer, even more the tongue of a prophet. Like a rudder that steers a big ship in the right direction, so is the tongue of a prophet that speaks from God's heart. Scripture says, "Or take ships as an example. Although they are so large and are driven by strong winds, they are steered by a very small rudder wherever the pilot wants to go. Likewise, the tongue is a small part of the body, but it makes great boasts. Consider what a great forest is set on fire by a small spark. The tongue is a fire, a world of evil among the parts of the body. It corrupts the whole body, sets the course of one's life on fire and is itself set on fire by hell" (James 3:4-5).

We need to learn how the anointing from Holy Spirit will operate in our own individual way. If we aspire to imitate another role model, we will reach a plateau. While respecting others who have gone before us, we need to learn how to walk in the anointing being our self. Holy Spirit teaches us these things as we walk out our days in authentic relationship with Him.

In our hunger to learn new things of God we can accept wrong teaching. I accepted some incorrect teaching that caused me problems. When Holy Spirit began to come upon me, I would visibly shake and find it difficult to speak as the power of God was upon me. Due to incorrect information I received from other believers, I did not question this manifestation. I believed that Holy Spirit was displaying His presence on me to others.

As I spoke with Holy Spirit about this matter, He showed me this passage in Scripture. "The spirits of prophets are subject to the control of prophets" (1 Corinthians 14:32). Holy Spirit showed me I was believing a lie that if I took control of my body, I would quench Him. I came to understand that as the power of God flows through me, I need to take control of my body to minister to people.

I was being controlled by a lie 25 years after Holy Spirit told me about how lies affect our decisions. Scripture said the spirit of the prophet is subject to the control of the prophet, yet I did not understand how this applied to my life. God showed me that in accepting the lie as truth, I had come out of agreement with His word. In response to this, I said to God, "I renounce the lie I have believed and come back into agreement with Your word, please forgive me." We must walk in agreement with the word of God or we will be led into error. As I was controlled by a misbelief, you can be controlled by a misbelief that will negatively affect you. It is essential for each of us to know God's Word and give Holy Spirit permission to reveal every way we are believing untruths preventing us from doing what God is calling us to do.

Know that we will each progress at different speeds. This is normal. If we start looking at the progress in others, we can allow discouragement to come into our lives. The timeline of each person's progress is unique. Trust God and be patient with His grace toward you on your learning journey.

Relationships are for a rcason, a season, or for life. As people in times of transition we may want to cling to the known. When repositioning occurs our comfort and understanding of what is correct will be challenged. For us to pick up what God has for us, we need to be willing to let go of things as God requires. Our obedience and trust in Him will be rewarded as we move into unfamiliar territory with Him.

Jesus has established the church through the first apostles and we are part of His church. We must come into alignment with His plan for prophecy as part of the five-fold ministry within His church. When the prophetic is in unity with the other four offices, there is great blessing to the body of Christ. Are you a church leader that desires to see the gift of prophecy operate in your meetings? Scripture tells us, "Follow the way of love and eagerly desire gifts of the Spirit, especially prophecy" (1 Corinthians 14:1). We are instructed by the apostle Paul to desire the gifts of the Spirit, especially prophecy. Whether a church leader or layperson, we are all learning to give a prophetic word, to receive a prophetic word, to test a prophetic word and to discover the meaning of a prophetic word.

Clear instruction about prophecy can bring about an environment where people respect each other while allowing prophecy to flow. It has been my experience that teaching on different aspects of this gift has brought greater harmony for the gift to operate. When the person teaching about prophecy understands how Holy Spirit communicates through us, they can help others to comprehend God's ways.

Understanding the nuances of walking in this gift is important in order to be a blessing to others. As people learn about prophecy, they will better understand how a word of prophecy is delivered and received. It is best to ask Holy Spirit for help first to understand any word you receive. People who interpret a word of prophesy strictly through their own understanding and the counsel of others may miss the meaning that God actually intended.

As a prophet, I have come to understand that prophecy is to be honoured as a gift to the body of Christ, a gift that brings life to believers. Holy Spirit will come upon people to prophesy in ways and at times that do not fit with your schedule. If we truly want Holy Spirit to move through prophecy in our services, we need to build freedom into the service for Holy Spirit to speak the message He places on the hearts of prophets.

The life of a prophet can be lonely as they are often misunderstood or feared. They can be perceived as odd to others as they speak words from God. Prophets need to be encouraged, especially by the leaders for being a blessing to the body of Christ. When a prophet needs correction, do it in private and be kind, remembering the person is in progress. As a leader, thank those operating in the gift of prophecy for the word of the Lord they bring.

A worship team helps the people in the service to experience the presence of God. God is pleased as the body of Christ comes together in unity, worshiping Him. In a service, Holy Spirit may want to move through prophecy. In order to flow with Holy Spirit, it is beneficial to expect words of prophecy being delivered. Ask your pastor or overseer how they want the worship team to respond as words of prophecy come. As a worship team, discuss this so that when a word comes you are prepared for its delivery. Additionally, discuss a format to be used when a member of the worship team has a word of prophecy to share as prompted by Holy Spirit. Ask Holy Spirit for wisdom to respond to words of prophecy in a way in which they will bless the body of Christ.

During my first experience of giving a corporate word, I began to speak out a word in tongues as a song was being sung in a service. I had not spoken in tongues previously, so I was shocked more than anyone. The worship leader recognized that a word of prophecy was being spoken in tongues. They stopped singing to allow the word to be spoken out. This is an example of how a word can come forth through a person who is unfamiliar with the power of Holy Spirit coming upon them. Discussion in advance however, will prepare you to flow with God and take the service to a higher level.

Several weeks prior to this occurring, a friend made a comment to me out of no-where. They said, if you ever get a word of prophesy in tongues, ask God for the interpretation. Well this did seem odd to me as I had not spoken in tongues yet, nor had I prophesied. In that moment when I spoke the word out in tongues, Holy Spirit brought back to my mind what my friend said. I acted on it, asking God for the interpretation of the word in tongues. As the pastor looked to me for the interpretation, I felt three words in my mind. This did not seem like a thorough interpretation, but I said, "Lord I will speak out what you give me as the interpretation." As I spoke out the three words in my mind, another 30 seconds of interpretation flowed out of me. Please hear this. God brought back to my remembrance the other person's comment to me. As He was faithful to help me, He will be faithful to help you. As I was very uncomfortable in speaking out this word and interpretation, you may be as well. Trust God to give you the words He wants spoken, He is faithful.

Each of us must go through the preparation process to get from where we are, to where we are called to be. We receive spiritual gifts from Holy Spirit as He wills. "All these are the work of one and the same Spirit and He distributes them to each one just as He determines" (1 Corinthians 12:11). Know that as you are teachable, that God can use you to operate in the gift of prophecy, regardless of your lack of earthly achievements such as education, title or position.

We have discussed how we should act in faith, speaking what God gives us to see God move. Through our obedience we can see God move through us to help and bless people in this world. It is a wonderful experience to allow Holy Spirit to flow through you in this gift revealing God's heart and purposes to people

Chapter 8

The Life of a Prophet

As a child of God walking in the gift of prophecy, we must give proper attention to our spirit, soul and body. We are a spirit in this world, we have a soul that is housed in our body. While we are on this earth, the house for our spirit is our body. We cannot extend our days on earth one second, but we can cut them short. How can we do this? Life choices. The way we care for our physical body.

In days gone by it was believed that as long as you were doing work for God, nothing bad would happen to you. We thought we could live any way we wanted without consequence. Scripture tells us it is God's will to heal us, but He has given us a responsibility to care for the health of our body. Our bodies are the temple of Holy Spirit and it is our responsibility to keep them healthy. "Don't you know that you yourselves are God's temple and that God's spirit dwells in your midst? If anyone destroys God's temple, God will destroy that person; for God's temple is sacred and you together are that temple" (1 Corinthians 3:16-17).

To live to our full potential, we will need the input of trusted people to help us in areas of our lives. As we study people who walked in great ministries in the past, we can learn from their lives. Some of these people suffered setbacks despite operating in powerful ministries. God tells us in Scripture, "My people are destroyed from lack of knowledge" (Hosea 4:6). If we dismiss what God tells us, we open ourselves up to consequences that could have been avoided.

Each of us needs the wise counsel of trusted people to see blind spots that require change. We need knowledge and understanding of the principles God has established. We find these principles in His word. God's principles work for us when we believe them and implement them in our lives. God said to forgive those who hurt us. As we choose to forgive, we close any doors that were open through un-forgiveness. Open doors are ways the evil one has to attach us physically, emotionally and mentally. We open doors for the enemy to attack us by not following the principles God has established. "See, I set before you today life and prosperity, death and destruction. For I command you today to love the Lord your God, to walk in obedience to him and to keep His commands, decrees and laws, then you will live and increase and the Lord your God will bless you in the land you are entering to possess" (Deuteronomy 30:15, 16). As we take time to learn about God's principles in His word and obey what God said to us in these principles, we will be blessed by Him.

Let me share this illustration with you. Gravity, which is part of creation, is constantly at work pulling things to the earth. As an example, gravity is pulling a plane to the earth every second of every day. The law of lift trumps the law of gravity, allowing the plane to leave the ground to fly, even though gravity remains in operation. Forgiveness is similar. When we make the choice to forgive, we exercise a higher law of God that frees us. Through forgiving we close the door on the enemy's ability to continue attacking us. This enables us to move beyond the pain caused by how others mistreated us. Forgiveness is a decision we choose to act upon, not a feeling we respond to.

Each of us needs to remember that God is provider. He knows our needs before we do. Jesus said, "Come to me, all you who are weary and burdened and I will give you rest. Take my yoke upon you and learn from me, for I am gentle and humble in heart and you will find rest for your souls. For my yoke is easy and my burden is light" (Matthew 11:28-30). Take Jesus at His word. Ask Him to remove burdens that are weighing you down and to give you rest for your soul.

Each of us is subject to the laws of nature on the earth. Walking in faith does not deny harsh realities in our lives. We do not deny that a mountain, representing a big problem stands before us. We do, however, believe in a higher reality, that being God. Through faith in

God, we pray, believing He will bring change to our circumstances.

As a person is trained to prophesy, the Lord will often work on the area of obedience. Our obedience includes prophetic acts. At times, such acts may seem unusual but can be powerful in breaking down strongholds. One well-known and powerful example of a prophetic act is found in Joshua 6. Instructions were given regarding how to take Jericho. The same God that told the Israelites to march around Jericho also told them to stand firm in the face of invading enemies. As they obeyed, they prevailed (2 Chronicles 20:15-22).

The prophet Jeremiah, was told to hide his girdle among some rocks. The girdle was destroyed by the water as a sign of how God was going to destroy the pride of Judah, (Jeremiah 13:1-11). These are two examples of how God asks us to act in faith in response to His word to us in ways that could seem very odd.

Obedience to God does not guarantee life will be easy or that we will find fulfillment for our soul. We must learn to do what God wants while not fretting over the struggle we have in doing it. "Now faith is confidence in what we hope for and assurance about what we do not see" (Hebrews 11:1). "Faith by itself, if it is not accompanied by action, is dead" (James 2:17). Walking by faith includes believing something and acting upon it. Some people who have been living by faith have seen great rewards while others have suffered greatly. Some did not receive what they were believing God for since God had something better planned for them.

Our words and actions must agree with what we are believing for. Many of us speak about faith, we hear about faith and read about faith. What is faith and what does it do for us? Scripture tells us that we please God when we act by faith. Faith by definition is complete trust or confidence in someone or something without proof. Therefore we please God when we trust Him without proof to back it up. We hear what He tells us in his word, we believe it and then act based on His word. We remain convinced about what He has said no matter what the circumstances look like.

Faith is the vehicle through which we receive that for which we have believed. We receive by asking God and believing He will give it to us. When we ask God for something, we need to expect that we will receive what we ask for. God tells us in His Word to ask and you shall receive (Matt 7:7). The goal of faith is to possess what we are hoping for. One example from Scripture involves two blind men. As Jesus was walking along two blind men who were following Him were calling out, "Have mercy on us." As Jesus went inside, they followed Him. Jesus asked them, "do you believe I am able to do this?" What was Jesus speaking of? He was referring to their request to give them their eyesight. The men responded to Jesus, "Yes Lord." Jesus touched their eyes and said to them, "according to your faith let it be done to you" (Matthew 9:27-31). Jesus looked for these men to respond to Him in faith for their request. Similarly, God looks to us to respond in faith to His prophetic word. These men followed Jesus, they called out to Him believing He could heal them. Their actions spoke of belief in Jesus ability.

Faith can operate either positively or negatively. With our words and actions we build faith to receive that for which we ask. As we focus on positive words and actions, we can bring positive things into our lives. Similarly, as we focus on negative words and actions, we can grow negative faith to bring negative things into our lives.

Have you ever wondered why negative things continue to come to those who focus on a negative outcome? The Word of God says, "Truly I tell you, if anyone says to this mountain, go throw yourself into the sea and does not doubt in their heart but believes that what they say will happen, it will be done for them. Therefore I tell you, whatever you ask for in prayer, believe that you have received it and it will be yours" (Mark 11:23-24). Through speaking to others of what we believe, we grow our faith to receive these things. As we speak words over and over, the expectation becomes stronger until we receive what we have been declaring. God said, that life and death is in the power of the tongue (Prov. 18:21).

In Scripture we see many instances where God called things that were not to be as though they were. As He did this, the power of His declaration and His positive faith brought about the change. And God said, "Let there be light and there was light" (Genesis 1:3). Was God telling the truth? Some would hear this statement and say it is untrue for what they see does not agree with what has been spoken. "The earth was formless and empty; darkness was over the surface of the deep" (Genesis 1:2). God called light to be, even though there was darkness present. Walking out the life of a prophet is done by faith. We listen to what God is speaking and we will repeat this.

To have a fruitful walk with God we need our faith increased. We feed our physical body 3 times a day even when we do not feel like it. Likewise, our faith needs to be fed through reading the Word of God. "Faith comes by hearing the message, and the message is heard through the word about Christ" (Romans 10:17).

Scripture tells us to come before God with thanksgiving for all He has done for us. To be successful we must look to Jesus as our example. When we react to the words or actions of another, we take Satan's bait. We have chosen to agree with the lie of the devil rather than what God has said. In the natural we understand how the words and actions of others hurt us.

If we are going to be successful in using the gift of prophecy, we must get our tongue under control. "Out of the same mouth come praising and cursing. My brothers and sisters, this should not be. Can both fresh water and salt water flow from the same spring? My brothers and sisters, can a fig tree bear olives, or a grapevine bear figs? Neither can a salt spring produce fresh water" (James 3:10-12). In this passage James is speaking of different things that should not co-exist in our speech. James speaks of how obviously salt water and fresh water cannot co-exist. In the same way, certain words should not co-exist in our speech. God is working to make us into a vessel through which His spirit can flow through without hindrance.

As a prophet we need to understand the purpose God has for us. Why did He give us this gift? The purpose of the prophetic gift is to speak encouragement, exhortation and comfort to people. If we are spending our time complaining or speaking badly about others, we have a conflict in our speech. We need to develop congruency in our speech so our words honour others whether we are prophesying or not. Ask God to help you avoid pointless conversations.

Our life should imitate the behaviour of Jesus. God will ask us to do things that stretch our understanding. Each of us needs to cooperate with Holy Spirit as He refines our character. Humility, by definition, is a modest view of one's own importance without pride or vanity present. We must always remember we are servants of the Lord and as His servants we must intentionally give God all the Glory. A humble person recognizes that it is God doing the supernatural work through them. They always thank God for what He has accomplished through them.

In John 9 Jesus heals a man born blind from birth in an unusual way. The disciples wonder who sinned, him or his parents since he was born this way. Jesus replied that it was for the Glory of God to be displayed that this happened. Jesus put mud on his eyes and told him to wash in the Pool of Siloam. It is interesting that He would tell a blind man to do this for he cannot see. However, as the man obeys Jesus and goes to the pool and washes, he receives his sight. In a similar way, God will ask us to do things that do not make sense in the natural, things that stretch our capacity to make sense and to obey.

Each of us needs to learn to obey what God asks us to do even when it does not make sense. As a disciple of Jesus Christ, we must be people growing in character. As we interact with other people, we need to be trustworthy and keeping our word. We need to take ownership of our mistakes and make amends where required. Be considerate to respect other people's time lines. Keep your word. When you promise something, do what you said you would. Give what you have determined to the church you attend. When called to help out in some way, do so with excellence.

Take time to deal with those areas of your life with which you struggle. A word of prophecy can be tainted by the issues one has in their own heart. Let us refer to Acts 8, the story of Simon the sorcerer. He received salvation, was baptized and was walking in this. For a long time before coming to salvation, Simon had impressed many with his sorcery but now he trusted his spiritual well being to Christ. However, although Simon was a Christian, he thought he could buy the gift of laying his hands on others so they could receive the spirit. Peter states the root of Simon's problem, "For I see that you are full of bitterness and captive to sin" (Acts 8:23). This former sorcerer had become a Christian but was still bound by iniquity. One example of being bound by iniquity could be manipulation, greed or control issues in a person's life that have been passed down through the generations.

When we are saved our spirit is redeemed and sealed by Holy Spirit. Our soul which is our mind, will and emotions is in progress towards full redemption. The unredeemed aspects in a person's life may continue to be heard as a prophet speaks. Holy Spirit enables us to speak mysteries and concepts that are beyond our natural mind or experience. To speak them more clearly ask God to reveal and redeem these areas that are negatively impacting the reception of what God is communicating. Because of what Jesus did on the cross, wounds can be healed and generational curses can be broken. Ask God for understanding to appropriate the work of the cross breaking the generational curse from your family line. As we do what Holy Spirit tells us to do, others will see Jesus in us more clearly.

To clarify, the way we treat others can reflect on God. If we are harsh, they could associate God being harsh toward them. If we refer to a person in some unedifying manner they could be offended and leave the church. Our actions, even on our own time, can reflect negatively on God.

It is amazing though that God uses us to speak His word in spite of our flaws. We represent God all the time, not just when we think we are. The devil is looking for us to act inappropriately so he can bring offense to others or condemnation to us. We are to love others in this world well. When we are mistreated we need to forgive. If we have mistreated anyone we need to sincerely apologize. Scripture tells us not to think of ourselves more highly then we should. Be gracious with those who have acted hurtfully toward you. Jesus told us that a disciple is not above their teacher. As much as it depends upon you, live at peace with others.

Chapter 9

Understanding Divine Revelation

Do words mean the same thing to God and to man? When we receive words of prophecy we need to be aware, they came from God and we need the help of Holy Spirit to unpack the meaning. The God of this universe continually entices us with mystery to draw us into greater fellowship with Him. He does not hide things from us. He hides things for us to discover. By pursuing Him for the deeper meaning of things we discover hidden treasures.

Elijah had run and hid in fear of Jezebel, who threatened to kill him. God in His mercy used it as an object lesson. Elijah received a greater revelation of who God is through this encounter. The Lord said, "Go out and stand on the mountain in the presence of the Lord, for the Lord is about to pass by" (1 Kings 19:11). As Elijah stood at the entrance to the cave where he had hidden, God passed by allowing Elijah to see some of His glory.

People communicate through words. The particular meaning of these words is learned through the culture in which we grew up in. We are influenced by our social position in that culture, the particular people who taught us as well as our personal frame of reference for that word. However, words can have quite a different meaning to God than they do to us. The God we serve is not bound by time, space, or dimension; He is infinite. To understand what is meant by a prophetic word from the Lord, it is ideal to ask Him for His meaning of the words spoken. Holy Spirit speaks to us individually based on who we are using words and terms that mean something to us. When we interpret a prophetic word based solely on our understanding of the words, we can be misled. We often conclude a word means what we think and so interpret the word that way. We need God to help us understand what He meant.

A word of prophecy coming into the natural is on God's timeline. As children of God we express our faith in the Prophetic Word by thanking Him for bringing it to pass before we see it. We need to apply our faith to the word as we receive the word of prophecy. Our posture is to remain optimistic that He is working all things together for our good as we endeavour to follow His purpose. "And we know that in all things God works for the good of those, who love Him, who have been called according to His purpose" (Romans 8:28). We read that He works for the good of those called, according to "His purpose." As we are in line with God's plan, we shall see Him empowering us to accomplish the work we are called to do.

We assume that prophetic words about time mean the same to God as they do to us. Take for example the word suddenly. It would seem to us that an event happened very soon after we hear the word suddenly. Normally speaking, there is a time of preparation leading up to the event taking place. Suddenly, on the day of Pentecost they all began to speak in other tongues. This came about over a period of many years according to God's plan. "And afterward, I will pour out my spirit on all people. Your sons and daughters will prophesy, your old men with dream dreams, your young men will see visions. Even on my servants, both men and women, I will pour out my Spirit in those days" (Joel 2:28-29). In this we see that what happened at Pentecost occurred many years after the word of prophecy was spoken. As humans we see the result of the manifestation of events described on the day of Pentecost. However, we rarely recognize the length of time God was at work behind the scenes bringing these events to fulfilment.

The word immediately was used by Jesus in this way. When the grain is fully ripe, then immediately the farmer comes and harvests it (Mark 4:29 KJV). What is called immediate is based on growth and preparation over time. The word now seems to be within a few hours. In reality, a farmer would need to align people and equipment to perform the harvest, which takes time. The important note here is to recognize that this is another word that can be misinterpreted. Immediately could mean from a few hours to a few weeks.

Early in King Saul's reign, he was given a word of prophecy from Samuel the prophet. "But now your kingdom will not endure, the Lord has sought out a man after His own heart and appointed him ruler of his people because you have not kept the Lord's command" (1 Samuel 13:14). Samuel told Saul that now his kingdom would not continue. It was many years later that the word "now" spoken by Samuel came about.

Jesus spoke these words. "Look, I am coming soon! My reward is with Me and I will give to each person according to what they have done" (Revelations 22:12). These words were spoken to the apostle John to write over two thousand years ago. Yet, we still wait for His return and He will return suddenly. This is another example of how terms about time can mean something very different to God than us.

Coming to a conclusion about the time frame in which we will receive what God has spoken can create another area of confusion. When God gives His word, He can fulfill His promise in the hours, days or years following and be completely correct. You may receive a prophetic word in which the Lord says, "I will do this immediately." Immediately would imply that the action is instantly going to occur. This is the meaning we as humans associate with this word. The result may not be received for a number of years. As God speaks to a person, He will work behind the scenes to bring about the fulfillment of His word. When we receive a word from the Lord, it is best to meditate on it. As we spend time with God, He will help us unpack what He meant about the time.

Holy Spirit is the one who leads us into all truth and understanding of prophecy. We cannot go to this place of understanding without faith. Faith is the vehicle that takes us where we want to go. Keeping an open mind is very important. Our enemy the devil wants us to become discouraged with a word of prophecy so that we will discard it. We must choose to believe God even when a word has not come to pass in the time we feel it should have. Thanking God for the word of prophecy is a way of responding in faith and expectancy.

Another example of words about time is when Jesus said; "The hour has come for the Son of Man to be glorified" (John 12:23). Jesus was speaking of the season or time in history for this to occur, not a specific time we would see on a clock.

The following are conversations recorded in Scripture between Jesus and other people. Jesus said something that was incorrectly interpreted by the people in each case. Jesus was teaching the people in the temple when the Pharisees asked Him what sign He would give to prove His authority. Jesus answered them, "Destroy this temple and I will raise it again in three days" (John 2:19). In this passage the Pharisees thought that Jesus was speaking of the physical Temple building. However, Jesus was referring to His earthly body, the temple in which He was residing during His time on earth. Although this was an understandable error, they missed the true meaning just the same.

Nicodemus, who was a member of the Jewish ruling council came to Jesus at night. He told Jesus that no one could perform the signs He was doing if God were not with him. Jesus replied, "Very truly I tell you, no one can see the kingdom of God unless they are born again" (John 3:2-3). Nicodemus concludes that Jesus is referring to a person being given physical birth a second time from their mother's womb. Jesus tells him "Flesh gives birth to flesh, but the Spirit gives birth to spirit" (John 3:6). In this example Nicodemus concludes that Jesus is speaking of the physical for this was his point of reference. Nicodemus was a learned man who taught others as a rabbi, yet he still did not comprehend the words of Jesus.

Another time Jesus was speaking with a Samaritan woman at a well when the disciples returned from buying food in town. They urged Him to eat. Jesus replied "I have food to eat that you know nothing about" (John 4:32). Hearing this the disciple's concluded He was speaking of food humans would eat, but Jesus said to them that His food was to do the will of Him who sent Him and to finish His work" (John 4:34). The disciples heard Jesus speak of food and concluded He was speaking of food humans consume to feed our body. Jesus was speaking of food as doing the will of the Father. In this example, we see Jesus was speaking on a spiritual level, while the disciples were understanding on an earthly level.

Jesus often spoke in parables, and we as humans, miss the meaning He intended. This caused people who really wanted the meaning to ask Jesus to explain the meaning. Our perspective is often limited to seeing the natural interpretation. It is wise to ask Holy Spirit for revelation, understanding and confirmation concerning these things. It seems God who is relational by nature wants to draw us into the mystery and exploration of deeper things. His methods take us deeper and include us pursuing Him for understanding of what He told us and us meditating on what he said.

Jesus even spoke this way to His disciples to draw them into closer relationship with Himself. These scriptural examples cited above demonstrate how God speaks and how we interpret what He has said. Often, we conclude something different than what God communicated to us. It is common for us to misunderstand God's intent. God, however, will continue to help us to understand His intent as we pursue Him.

A prophetic word is spoken by God through another person communicating important information to us. By us pursuing Him for more understanding, He draws us into greater relationship with Himself. To interpret the prophetic message, we need God's assistance. We should not assume that what we think a word means is what God intends. God tells us in Isaiah 55:9, that His ways are as high above our ways as the heavens are above the earth. If we jump to a conclusion about the meaning of words, we can miss the real meaning God intended. I recommend that you utilize the Word of God and ask Holy Spirit for wisdom to comprehend the meaning of a prophetic word. Honour Holy Spirit by making Him the first one you ask for help, every time. The word of God is a plumb line that we can use to measure if a word of prophecy is from Him.

Wisdom would see us seeking out born again, spirit filled believers, for assistance in understanding what God means. Look for those who regularly receive revelation from God through pictures, images, or words from God. To receive the complete revelation we need to clearly hear from Holy Spirit ourselves.

We see in the Biblical account in Luke 2, an example of the fulfillment of prophecy about Jesus. Joseph and Mary took Jesus to the temple to present Him before God. There they encountered Simeon. Simeon was a devout man waiting for the consolation of Israel and

Holy Spirit was on him. Moved by the Spirit he had come into the temple courts as the parents brought Jesus in. Simeon recognized the baby Jesus as the promised Messiah. On the same occasion, a prophetess named Anna recognized that the baby Jesus was the promised Messiah as revealed to her by Holy Spirit. For both Simeon and Anna, Holy Spirit gave them revelation that Jesus was the Christ, prophesied about.

In this world we acquire intellectual knowledge, experiential knowledge and revelation knowledge about God. Intellectual knowledge is information we know in our own mind, that we have read about God. Experiential knowledge is information gained from an intimate walk with God. Revelation knowledge is information we receive directly from God and the most impactful on our walk as a believer. This information is given to us by God to enable us to live as a child of God. Revelation knowledge will stick with us and not be shaken by testing or challenges from other people. This gives us an understanding of God that no other person could. Revelation knowledge takes us much deeper in our understanding of God. Information we learn from man can be challenged, debated and discounted. Revelation knowledge from God will not be shaken or discounted through any means. Revelation knowledge equips us to know, that we know, that we know, what we received is true. No attempt of the devil will be able to erode this truth that God has revealed to us. Anything we claim to be true in life will be tested, in an effort to discount what we received. Revelation knowledge is a by-product of an intimate relationship between us and God.

The revelatory realm comprises the ways God communicates with His people. These are the audible voice of God, the still small voice of God, an impression, a sudden thought, an open vision, a closed vision, a dream, word of Scripture coming to life, God speaking through nature, our surroundings or other people. This is a list of the primary ways God speaks, although this is not an exhaustive list.

As we begin operating in the gift of prophecy it is necessary to recognize the different ways God communicates with us. God communicates with each of us uniquely, although He may use the same ways with different people. The audible voice of God would be hearing God with our ears as we would another human being. The still small voice of God is where we hear God in our spirit or our mind.

An impression is where we sense God giving us knowledge about a situation we knew nothing about. When we receive an impression, we know confidently what is correct, yet have no way to prove it. This knowledge comes without any effort on our part, and is often referred to as a knowing about something.

A sudden thought, that interrupts the natural flow of our thinking, can seem like a random thought that pops into our mind when we do not expect it. It could seem like our mind was wandering to think on things other than what we were focused on. As an example, we could be driving down the street and the thought comes to call someone. These thoughts come as a result of God prompting us to act on behalf of another that has some need.

An open vision is where we would see a vision in front of us with our eyes open. This could be fully three dimensional, even more real then what we see in life. A closed vision would be seeing a vision in our minds eye. Both of these visions are communications from God and equally legitimate. Although closed vision is the most frequent way God speaks, it is wise to remain open to any way He communicates with us. A dream is something we experience during our sleep where God speaks to us through symbols. Words of Scripture coming to life happens when reading or listening to Scripture. Words seem to jump off the page as we read them or come alive as we hear them. These words of Scripture touch us in a significant way that is impactful.

God speaking through nature would encompass us sensing God speak to us through something in this world that cannot speak. It could be a sign along the road, a field of hay, trees in a forest, an animal or clouds in the sky as examples. As we are open to God speaking to us through any means He wants, we will expand our ability to hear, see and sense things from Him.

We are living in a season where the prophetic is coming alive in many people. Knowing God's Word is more important now than ever. "All Scripture is God-breathed and is useful for teaching, rebuking, correcting and training in righteousness, so that the servant of God may be thoroughly equipped for every good work" (2 Timothy 3:16-17). To walk in the gift of prophecy we must believe His word. We cannot choose what parts of His word we will believe and what we will not.

"They will turn their ears away from the truth and turn aside to myths" (2 Timothy 4:4). We read that people will walk away from the truth and pursue others who will tell them what they want to hear. They will receive sayings of people that have traces of God's Word, appearing to be correct, but are lies of the devil. By knowing what Scripture tells us, we will be equipped to discern what is true and what is false in this world.

God said, "I the Lord do not change" (Malachi 3:6) and "Surely the Sovereign Lord does nothing without revealing His plan to his servants the prophets" (Amos 3:7). In this we see God reveals what He is planning to do through His prophets. People are hungrier to hear from God now than ever. This hunger can direct a person to make choices that lead them into error. They can receive teaching that sounds good, but is incorrect because they have no basis to discern what is correct. As we apply ourselves to know God's Word, and receive practical instruction in Godly principles, we can be equipped to detect and avoid deception. God wants to give us greater understanding, but man's pride in what he knows and ignorance make him vulnerable to deception.

"God is not human, that He should lie, nor a human being, that He should change His mind. Does He speak and then not act? Does He promise and not fulfill" (Numbers 23:19). The prophet Balaam tells us that God will do what He said. He is not like man who changes his mind and lies about matters. We can count on God to keep His word spoken to us. As we keep embracing the promises of God, we may battle doubt, and we may struggle to keep trusting until we receive the answer to our prayers. A person does not need to understand the promises of God to have them work for them, they must believe them. By knowing what God did in the past, we can better understand what He would do now.

God plants seeds that will grow as we read His word, seeds that will give us insight into the heart of God. The enemy knows this and so he plants seeds of doubt. We can receive great insight into God's Word as we regularly read and meditate on it. We protect ourselves from false teaching by knowing His word and treasuring it in our heart. The more of God's Word we commit to our heart, the less prone we will be to being led astray. Through Old Testament we can learn about God's principles. We can claim all the promises God made to Abraham through Jesus Christ.

God has given us laws, principles and promises to live by. These are present both in the spirit and in the natural. Let me share an illustration with you. Gravity is a force on earth that remains constant. The law of gravity is in place every moment of every day. It does not stop operating nor does the law of gravity change. If this is so, how does a plane leave the ground? Gravity is pulling the plane to the ground every moment of every day. There is a greater law in place, the law of lift. By creating wings on a plane with a greater wing surface on top than on bottom, a lower pressure area is created above the wing.

As the plane moves forward down the runway, this lower pressure gives the plane lift to leave the ground and fly. Although the law of gravity does not stop operating, the law of lift overrides the law of gravity. Both are in operation simultaneously, yet one is greater than the other. God has given us the law of prayer to trump the work of the devil. When we pray, decree and declare according to the Word of God, our prayer will bring changes to our circumstances. Through our prayers, God protects us by thwarting Satan's efforts. Through thanking God for answering our prayer before we receive it, we exercise our faith, moving to a place of belief and trust in God.

As we obey God and His word, we shall receive what we ask for in prayer. Jesus said, "Very truly I tell you, whoever believes in me will do the works I have been doing and they will do even greater things than these, because I am going to the Father. And I will do whatever you ask in my name, so that the Father may be glorified in the Son. You may ask me for anything in my name and I will do it" (John 14:12-14). In this passage of Scripture Jesus tells us that He will give us what we ask for when we pray in His name. To receive we must believe God will give us what we ask for. As we believe God's word and pray in the name of Jesus, we come at the enemy with the authority of Jesus. As we pray, God is able to overrule the work of the devil. Therefore, the devil will use many tactics to keep us from prayer. He will even give us good things to do so we do not have time to pray. Why would the devil do that? It is because of the great power that is released by God when we pray.

When we pray in tongues it is even more devastating for the enemy because he does not understand what is spoken. You may have noticed as you reflect on how you were going to spend time with God that the phone would ring, someone would knock on the front door, a child would call you, fill in the blank for your life. The devil uses these tactics to keep you occupied so you will not be able to spend that time with God in prayer.

Partnering with God requires a choice on our part. We must choose to do what God wants and say no to the distractions that come our way. You may feel there are things you must do. The only way to know for certain what God wants is to get quiet before Him and listen. As we listen, He will show us what He wants us to do. God is on a relentless pursuit of us so that we can experience the full life he desires for us as His children. Our flesh and the devil are competing for our attention to prevent us from pursuing God.

In this chapter we looked at different ways people heard a message from God and incorrectly interpreted the meaning. Each of us needs the assistance of Holy Spirit to understand what is communicated through a word of prophecy.

Chapter 10

Intimacy with God

How do we grow in intimacy with God? Intimacy comes through us spending time with and us surrendering to God. From when we invite Jesus into our hearts, till we die, our journey of surrender progresses. When we surrender to God, we admit that we cannot do things on our own and accept His help through the gift of salvation. From that point until we die, we can grow into deeper intimacy as we will admit to God that we need Him.

Holy Spirit is our teacher who reveals truth to us as we are willing to learn. We improve by having God show us what is true. This is an ongoing process of God renewing our mind. Do not allow your mindset to become your blind set. Will we allow the need to be right, to rob us of the opportunity to learn from God? Jesus said, "But when the Spirit of truth comes, He will guide you into all the truth. He will not speak on His own, He will speak only what He hears and He will tell you what is yet to come" (John 16:13). He also said, "For those who are led by the Spirit of God are the children of God" (Romans 8:14). We are the children of God and Holy Spirit is the Spirit of Truth, our teacher.

Do we believe that Holy Spirit is able to teach us? I encourage you to ask Him to teach you what you need to learn. When I am unsure of something, I will ask Holy Spirit a question like this. "Lord, I do not understand what I am to do. Will you help me? Give me wisdom so that I will comprehend what you are telling me. Thank you, Lord."

The bible has been broken down by man into chapters and verses for ease of reading. The original text was not this way, but each book was one continuous letter. As we read Scripture pursuing truth, we need Holy Spirit to help us understand God's Word. When we incorrectly interpret Scriptures, we place ourselves in error. One needs wisdom to apply the Word of God to determine what He said and what He meant. Taking a few words of a Scripture to support our belief is incorrect. We must include all the verses that are related to the thought being spoken about. As well, understanding the context and cultural relevance can assist in correctly interpreting and understanding Scriptures.

We need Holy Spirit to teach us to come into agreement with His word more today than yesterday. We do this as we allow Him to teach us the meaning of Scripture. Who do we allow to speak into our lives? Some people speak of God's Word, yet follow their own understanding. When we claim to follow God yet do our own thing, we mislead ourselves. The choices we make in living our life reflects what we believe. For us to walk successfully as a prophet we must be willing to look at every part of our life. Do our choices align with the standard of God's Word? Do I cooperate with the changes God wants to bring in me? Do we own our poor choices so we can mature in our walk as a child of God? I encourage you to read this prayer and if you are willing, speak it to God. God said this day I set before you life and death, choose life.

God, I give myself to you. Holy Spirit, take hold of my life. Align me with the will of God. Use me in your kingdom. Teach me what I need to learn. Help me become teachable. I want what you have for me. I consecrate my life to you. Help me learn to hear you and obey you in all I do. In Jesus name.

When we hear from Holy Spirit, we have a choice to make. Our natural mind may tell us what we heard is nonsense. Our mind and rational thinking are often opposed to things being spoken by the Spirit. If it does not make sense our mind says it cannot be true or good. The things of the Spirit are discerned by the Spirit. Doubt often rises in our minds because of our desire to logically understand things of the Spirit. This is the part where people talk themselves out of delivering or receiving a word of prophecy. I have found the need to understand things with my intellect a hindrance. If we will speak out quicker than we can think, we will disarm doubt that logical thinking brings.

Our spirit knows that what we heard came from Holy Spirit. To progress forward we need to say yes to Holy Spirit, doing what He said to do. We must become intimately acquainted with the voice of Holy Spirit. This requires that we set aside other activities so we can listen to what The Spirit wants to tell us. Holy Spirit longs for us to know Him personally. The Spirit of God desires a relationship where we recognize He is God, who wants to teach us, and instruct us about all things.

Throughout my day I listen for His voice to hear what He has to tell me. When I go to bed, the last thing I do is say, "Good night Holy Spirit." As I am going through my day I hear from Holy Spirit as He highlights a thought that another person is speaking to me, words jumping off a page, or a thought dropping into my mind. When I sense He is speaking to me I will note what was highlighted to me. I will write it down to record it. When there is an opportunity, I will ask Him the meaning of what came to my mind. I will ask Him for wisdom to comprehend what He has spoken to me.

I do not accept everything that is attributed to have come from God. I ask Holy Spirit if what was implied to come from Him did or not. If it did, I ask for clarification. When we accept any thing someone tells us as a word from God, we can be led into confusion. Not everything a person thinks comes from God, is actually from God. Test the Spirits.

When we tell Holy Spirit we will do something, do we follow through keeping our word? How do we honour Him in our day? He wants us to include Him in everything. Not just the spiritual part of our lives, but every part. He wants us to include Him in the interesting, the mind numbing, the possible and the impossible things we face. Holy Spirit even wants us to include Him in the most intimate parts of our lives, allowing Him into every room of our life.

Holy Spirit will communicate with us through different methods including prophetic words, dreams and visions. God is the author of the message that is communicated in these ways and so God must be involved for us to understand the meaning of the message. When we receive a dream, a vision, or a prophetic word, we should record the details of this on paper or an audio device. The first one we speak with about these details should be Holy Spirit. As we do this, we show by our action that He is our source. God's counsel needs to be the priority in our life, confirmation can come from others. On our journey in interpreting and understanding God's message, ideally, we increase in depending on God for insight as we grow. Personally, I discuss with Him what I experienced, and what it seems to mean to me. I include Holy Spirit in all the details, even the small details that appear insignificant. As we interact with Holy Spirit, He will walk us through the process of correctly unpacking what was communicated to us through the words and images.

The Spirit of God is the author of all prophecy and so He will help us understand what He intended to tell us. He may direct us to another person or resource to gain understanding, but we need to make Him our first stop. When we go to Him first, we show by our actions that we believe He is our teacher. Holy Spirit is the God representative here on earth and so we need to interact with Him as such. In following this practice, we will receive greater understanding into the prophetic words, dreams and visions than we ever have before. For us to move into a more intimate place of relationship with God we need to learn more about being vulnerable.

It seems each of us is uncomfortable being transparent with God. The truth is that God knows everything about us including our flaws before we say a word. "Search me, God and know my heart, test me and know my anxious thoughts" (Psalm 139:23). King David said to God, search me and know me, show me if there be any wicked way in me. Are we willing to be this exposed with God? Will we give Holy Spirit permission to place his finger on what needs His touch? How do we respond as Holy Spirit points out an area needing change? Growing in intimacy requires time and vulnerability. God knows all about us yet He wants to be part of everything we do in our life.

Deep relationship is where people share all of their lives together. They allow each other to know all that is going on in their life, speaking honestly as with a friend. Do we call Holy Spirit our friend?

If we call Him our friend, how do we treat Him? We can offend Him with our words. Do we avoid speaking about difficult topics? People wonder why they do not see the power of God flowing through them, but do they ask God why. I believe it has to do with the degree to which we will face out heart issues. He is the spirit of truth. We were not asked to come to God with our life together. No, God asks us to come. He will help us get our life together.

Each of us must learn to recognize Holy Spirit's presence. We need to recognize Him since sometimes He comes on us in power. Recognizing the voice and presence of Holy Spirit should become natural to us. As we go through our day, He is with us and speaks to us. As He comes upon us He makes us aware that He is there. As He speaks to us, we need to recognize the ways He speaks. As we open our selves up to Holy Spirit, He will help us grow in these areas. Sensing Him, listening to Him and partnering with Him are keys to greater intimacy with Holy Spirit.

Each person has a responsibility to their family, the community of believers they regularly attend and their employer. To walk with God, we need to keep the correct balance of time and focus in each of these areas. We need to balance the time we spend in each area according to their importance. We need to regularly attend the community of believers that we can be encouraged and to encourage others as well. Each person has a call on their life to do the work of ministry. Each of us needs to balance out the ministry work we are called to and what we are to do as part of the community of believers. Each of us needs to determine what God has called us to and do that in balance with other responsibilities.

Here is an example of my experience in growing in intimacy, I will share about this book. I felt God speak to me to write a book. At first, I felt this would be great. It was a stage of adventure and exhilaration. But, then I thought I am not very good at the English language, how can I do this, my insecurities and doubts rose to the surface. For several weeks I pondered this thought. Then I told Colleen my wife what I though God was telling me to do. She was very affirming and supportive. I looked on the Internet about how to write a book to get an idea. Then I began to write, but I had no theme. Hmm, how could I write a book without a theme? I asked God, "What should I be writing this book about?" He replied, "Prophecy." So, I thought to myself, I can do this since I have learned a bit and read books on the subject. I did not realize it then but as I began stepping into what God asked me to do, He was teaching me to think more like Him. So, I began the process of recording information I felt was related to prophecy for the next few weeks. Then, I hit a wall. I was overwhelmed with thoughts that I could not do this.

In a moment of frustration, I deleted all the information I had gathered. For the next week I went about my business when suddenly I felt Holy Spirit say, "Steve, how is that book coming?" Boy, did I feel like a deer caught in the headlights. I said, "Lord, you know all things, you already know that I deleted everything as I was frustrated." Then, Holy Spirit said, "But I asked you to write it." Again, I gave Him some excuse for not doing it. Again, He came back with a kind but firm response, "But I asked you to write it." I asked Him if He had considered asking my wife Colleen to write it. I pointed out that she could speak and write far better than I could. Again, He replied (I could sense Him smiling), "I asked you to write it." I realized that excuses and deflection did not work for Moses and they were not going to work for me either. At this point I did not know what to do, so I tried to make a deal with Him. I said, "Lord I will do it under one condition." He asked me, "What is that?" I said, "You must help me. How can I a mere human write about divine truths I know nothing about? I know a few things you have taught me but I am not able to teach others about you in a book." Then, Holy Spirit said, "Deal. I will help you." I felt Him chuckle as He said these words to me. That was all He said and I felt He meant it so I began the journey again. I found myself wondering, would Holy Spirit really say, "deal?" Somehow this did not fit the mould I had for how He would answer.

Before moving forward this time, I stopped and spoke with Holy Spirit. I said, "Lord how should I go about writing this book? Holy Spirit, I invite you into the process of writing this book and I ask you to help me." Immediately I saw in my minds eye a blank sheet of paper. Then on the top of the sheet a few words were written on it, forming a thought. Then I saw writing begin to appear that expanded this thought. As this occurred, I felt Him speak to me so soft and gently, "I will give you a thought to write about. Take that thought and expand it to say what I show you." After He said this, I saw the same sheet of paper with the thought on the top and several paragraphs of expansion on this thought. He spoke to me again, "Steve, then we will take another thought and we will do the same. After we get enough thoughts we will put them together to make a chapter. When we have enough chapters, we will put them together to make a book." Wow, was I amazed at how clearly Holy Spirit showed me how to write this book. I realized He was showing me that He could teach me anything I needed.

Now that I was beginning to understand this, I began to write the book. I seemed to bounce around in identifying what to write about and what the chapters should contain. What should I call each chapter? What should I call this book? In spite of not knowing these things, I choose to move forward in whatever way I could, trusting that He would help me as He said He would. As I took steps of faith, I would have thoughts come to my mind that answered questions I had. For the next few months I began to brainstorm writing down every thought I felt could be relevant to this book.

After about 6 months I began to sort the different thoughts into categories that were to become chapters. As I was getting the thoughts corralled into chapters I began to sift through the chapters to eliminate superfluous information. During this process I felt Holy Spirit speak to me about points to include. These ideas would come through listening to another person, watching TV, listening to a sermon, listening to music, or feeling an impression from Holy Spirit. He showed me that He can and will speak to us in varied ways. He is teaching me to hear Him in whatever way He speaks to me. Each of us is different. We hear from God differently and process thoughts differently. Therefore, we must walk out what God is asking us to do in the unique way that works for us.

Now, as I was writing this book, I would let trusted people in a bit here and there. I was feeling very vulnerable about being criticized by others who did not agree with what I wrote. God was showing me that I had a voice. I realized God wanted me to write the book to have my perspective on the writing. If He wanted to have someone else's perspective, He would have asked them to write it.

As I have continued to walk out writing this book, I have continued to gain momentum. God has brought more people into my life to give me guidance as I walk out this journey. I share my journey to show you that when He asks us to do something, He will help us. Our response is to take the first step of faith. Then begin working at what we are asked to do, engaging Him in the process. Any of us can sit back and say I cannot do this for it is bigger than me.

If God asks us to do something that we can do on our own, we have no need of Him. By Him asking us to do something that is far bigger than we are capable of doing, we are forced to rely on Him. We learn how to interact with Holy Spirit in doing something practical in this world. Holy Spirit is totally capable of teaching us and helping us do anything He asks us to do. On this writing journey I did hit walls at several points and found myself exasperated. My natural reaction was to delete the book and give up. However, even in these valleys, I never doubted that God would help me as He had promised at the start of this book-writing journey.

Has He asked you to do something you have dismissed? If so, speak to Him about this. Ask Him to forgive you for not being obedient. Ask Him to help you. Admit your inability to do what He has asked you to do. As you humble yourself, He will begin teaching you to think in a new way. I assure you He is faithful. He will show you ways to do what He has asked you to do that will amaze many. As Holy Spirit has helped me, He will help you as well.

God asks us to do something to get the flavour of our personality in what we do. God will empower us to do what He asks us to do. You can do all things through Christ who strengthens you, (Phil 4:13). Another reason is we learn much more about God as we pursue something where we are completely reliant on Him. When we know we cannot do it on our own, we will more easily see when God is at work helping us.

God said, "Go and make disciples of all nations." If what we are doing is not leading people to Christ and taking believers to a higher level in their maturity, we may be off base.

As a person walking in the gift of prophecy it is key, we hear from the Lord. We will see more accomplished by us speaking a single anointed word from Holy Spirit at the correct time than all our self-efforts. We need to let go of any illusion that we can accomplish anything in our own strength. We need to understand that Holy Spirit is God. He knows all things including those things hidden in the heart of God.

We must be in regular communication with Jesus to stay in the right place doing the right thing for His plan. Our adversary the devil will speak partial truths through any person, even believers that will allow him to. That is impossible you say. Do you remember when Jesus spoke to His disciples of His needing to die on the cross? Peter rebuked Jesus saying, "that will never happen." What did Jesus say? He rebuked Satan who was speaking through Peter. On earth Peter was one of the closest people to Jesus. If Peter can be used of the devil, through unbelief, any of us can be used as well. For us to think we are above that, we are out of touch with our humanity. We can rebuke the devil in Jesus name but in our self, we are no match for the devil. We must remain in Christ to stand against all the ways the devil wants to deceive us.

We can claim to be dying to self and yet continue in our own path. A place of continual surrender is needed to walk in victory. When we are in line with the plan Jesus has for us, fruit will be evident. He will bless everything we do because it is His plan. If you do not know how to do what the Lord asks you to do, ask Him. When we are following God's plan, He will direct our steps. He will teach us what to do and how to do it. He is for us! Doing the work of the Lord should be a joy not a burden. For any of us to go deeper in God we need to want relationship with God as a priority. We must want to please God more than we want to please man. This means walking in obedience and surrender to Him.

We cannot fulfill the plan of God unless we submit to Him and His will. This will require that we let go of things that are preventing us from doing what God wants us to do. These things we need to let go of could be power, position, money, possessions, relationships, time, our plan, our aspirations, our reputation, ambition, ministry work, lies and mindsets to name a few. God will place His finger on the issue in our life that He wants to deal with. It is not enough for us to want to be closer to God, we must do what God is showing us to do. We must want His help to let go of things we are distracted by; He will not trump our free will.

I will share an example of how Holy Spirit communicated a point to me in a way that challenged my understanding of Him. As I was going through my day at work, I was walking down the hall when in my minds eye I saw a snakes and ladders game board appear. As it came into view I asked, "Holy Spirit, is that you? Are you wanting to tell me something?" He said, "Yes Steve, I want to show you something. On the snakes and ladders board the snakes represent a negative event and the ladders represent a positive event. These are representative of life. You cannot do anything without me. You must be in step with me to do what I have called you to do. If you run off ahead or if you lag behind you are out of step with me. If you are ahead or behind me, you cannot do what you are to do. In order to do what I have called you to do you must be in step with me. I work through circumstances to speed you up or to slow you down, getting you in step with me to accomplish what I have called you to do at the correct time. Do not look at circumstances that alter your position as positive or negative, but rather an adjustment of your position. As you cooperate with me, I can adjust your position more easily." This was certainly a new way of looking at Snakes and Ladders. God was giving me a higher perspective through a familiar object.

This event was revealed to me over two days. As I thought about what I believed Holy Spirit had spoken, I asked Him, "Lord, did you really use the Snakes and Ladders board as an illustration tool? I can hardly believe you would have done that." He replied, "Yes, Steve, I did. I will use many different ways to communicate with you. Do not miss what I am speaking due to the method I use to communicate. I use these methods to enable you to understand the message I am speaking to you." I learned that I should not dismiss what Holy Spirit communicates because of the words or the illustrations He chooses to use. I must learn to recognize life teachings He reveals to me, as He draws me into deeper relationship with Him. God often speaks creatively and draws upon our curiosity.

Chapter 11

Perfecting the Gift

To perfect any gift in life one must regularly operate in the gift. The gift of prophecy is no different. We will discover, to grow in the gift of prophecy we need to exercise the gift of prophecy. Each of us develops as we step out in faith speaking the word of prophecy given to us by Holy Spirit.

An athlete trains each day to improve their performance. The athlete makes changes to their life, throwing off anything that would impede them from reaching the goal. They evaluate and make changes to their training and diet to achieve peek performance. They take preventative measures to minimize the chance of injury although they recognize it could occur. As they develop, they accept the reality of pain, sacrifice and setbacks being part of being an athlete. They listen to and apply the wise counsel of their coach, trainer and physician in order to reach the end goal of winning. Every athlete recognizes that listening to wise counsel will help them to achieve the greatest success.

An athlete balances exercise, diet, rest, family and social life in their lives to survive the long journey to the podium. It is imperative that an athlete keep their eyes on the end goal in order to press through situations that could cause them to quit. An athlete remains focused on the prize of winning. Quitting is not an option that is entertained. Similarly, a prophet needs to operate in the prophetic gift daily to improve their ability. A person must adjust their lifestyle so they can walk in this gift. They must be willing to make any changes required to grow in this gift.

One must become intentional about spending time with Holy Spirit.

He speaks to us in different ways and settings. We need to learn to hear Him in the different ways and settings He speaks. As an athlete throws off anything that hinders them, we must be willing to throw off what would hinder us from developing in this gift. Incorrect ways of thinking hold us back. God wants us to live out of truth. Become willing to throw off anything that hinders you, including your beliefs. We have several categories of beliefs pertaining to ourselves, others, God and circumstances. Aligning ourselves with truth in each of these areas will assist us in becoming who God wants us to be and achieve His purpose for us. Choose to ask Holy Spirit to show you anything in your belief system that is not true. For a person to grow in their ability to hear Holy Spirit they must include Him as they go through their day. As you go through your day listen for Him to speak to you. Pursue clarification about what He told you and then do what He told you to do.

As a prophet matures, they understand they will be hurt by people who they interact with. God wants to refine and heal our character even in this. In order to thrive in the journey, we need to follow the guidelines God gave us in His word. We do this as we shake off the hurts encountered, not taking offense and forgiving those who hurt us. Encounters with other believers may also be used to refine and help us. Scripture tells, "As iron sharpens iron, so one person sharpens another" (Proverbs 27:17).

In leaning on our own understanding, we can find ourselves, like Elijah, under our own broom tree. After feeling attacked we can pull away from people who hurt us. We may explain to God why we cannot do this anymore as we have been beaten up once too often. God takes us through circumstances to cause things in us that are not of Him to die.

It is my experience that some of these moments can be extremely painful as we feel our world is crumbling. There will be times we shall feel like our whole life is being turned inside out. We may be so significantly affected by negative emotion that we are not sure who our friends are any more. In these moments we may loose perspective, but we must choose to trust God. As He takes us deeper in Him, He will take us through challenges of life where He encourages us to trust more deeply in Him.

As we step out in faith, we will make mistakes. This is a reality of learning. Do not let this stop you from giving a word from the Lord. As a person begins, Holy Spirit will teach them many different things. A prophet will learn to recognize Holy Spirit speaking in unfamiliar terms and situations. Holy Spirit is very fluid in how He operates as there is no formula in prophecy.

Growing into a higher level in the gift of prophecy requires that our daily conduct be examined. Every part of our lives is to display integrity. Be a person that others can count on, one who follows through when they give their word to do something. Ephesians 5 contains instructions about how we are to act, live and speak. As children of God we are to display these behaviours for the world to see. We are to live lives as dearly loved children of God. Our lives should model the way of love as Christ lived. There should not be obscenity, foolish talk, or coarse joking in our speech. Rather, we should speak words of truth, love and kindness to others. Be people who speak words of life into others. Our conduct should be such that others come to us for guidance. For us to achieve this, we need to measure our conduct against the standard of God's Word. God gives us the grace and power for us to change.

When we give our word to do something, follow it through to completion. Speak honestly with others and let your yes be yes and your no be no. Learn to stand by your convictions even when others disagree and yet with grace and respect, value the opinions of others. Allow God to shape you so you become confident speaking what He tells you.

Since God is Spirit, we are to worship him in spirit and truth. This can only be done with the assistance of Holy Spirit. To worship in spirit and truth is to come before God of our own free will. We worship the Father with all our being by our own choice. We allow Holy Spirit to flow through us so that we can enter into worship of God whole-heartedly. As we worship God, we give of ourselves to Him. Allow your emotions to be expressed to God as you worship Him, letting Him into your heart. At the same time we are worshiping Him we receive from Him. As we come before the Father in thanksgiving and worship, we move His heart to bless us.

Jesus spoke to the Samaritan woman at the well about worshiping the Father in Spirit and in truth. In the Old Testament the way people worshipped, was with all their might fulfilling the law. To receive all that is available to us we need to align our praise and worship according to the Word of God. This includes our praise and worship flowing out of a thankful heart. All of our life is worship. As we grow in faith and experience, we live with an attitude of gratitude and thanksgiving.

Everything we have has come from God. What we will give back to God is an indication of our level of trust in Him. At the cross Jesus took the curse upon Himself for all. This includes the curse that came upon people for not giving a tithe back to God in the Old Testament. If we want to receive a greater harvest, we must learn that being generous in giving is key. This applies to what we give back to God through the many ways we give. These ways include giving our money, time, abilities, possessions etc. We can take the position that we are under grace and do not have to give to the church. When we adopt this kind of mindset, we miss out on the blessings God has for us.

Living as a disciple of God requires that we yield our will to His will doing what He tells us to do. There is a big difference between being a born-again child of God and being a disciple of God. We should not give to get. God does not do this, we should not either. "Each of you should give what you have decided in your heart to give, not reluctantly or under compulsion, for God loves a cheerful giver" (2 Corinthians 9:7). Our giving should be done from a place of thankfulness for all God has done for us. We should decide in advance what we are going to give on a regular basis. Then, on special occasions ask God what He wants us to give in those instances. As we live as a disciple of Jesus, we will honour God. Everything we have is God's. We need to learn to hold earthly resources loosely. Freely giving are indicators of mature stewardship of what God has given us. With a grateful heart we interact with other people in our sphere of influence.

We need to understand Holy Spirit is God and able to do what He wants, when He wants. Holy Spirit is the third person of the trinity.

He is equally God as the Father is God and Jesus is God. The Father, Jesus and Holy Spirit are in agreement about the plan of redemption for man in this world. Holy Spirit will speak through us to others according to the will of God. As we begin to comprehend how capable Holy Spirit is, we realize He will make us aware when He wants us to do something for Him.

At first, I struggled with understanding how He would make me aware of what He wanted me to do. I realized I was viewing Him as a human. Through regular interaction with Holy Spirit, He makes me aware of what He wants me to do. Coming to terms with issues like this empowers us to see Holy Spirit operate through us. As we grow in the prophetic gift, it is common to see the word of knowledge and the word of wisdom gifts utilized with a word of prophecy. I will share some examples of ways Holy Spirit has operated through me in different ways and settings to help illustrate this.

Here are several examples of how Holy Spirit comes upon me in my day to speak a word to another person. As I go through my day, He comes upon me when I am aware and other times when I am not aware. There are times He will speak through me in an obvious manner, other times in a less obvious way. As I have come to understand His ways, I have become more relaxed as I live my life.

On one occasion I was speaking with a person at work, whom I will call Sally, not their real name. Sally had injured her knee playing sports and needed a cane to walk. As we conversed, I asked Sally if I could pray for God to heal her knee. She said I could. So, in a low-key manner I said, "Father, I ask you to heal Sally's knee from the injury, remove all pain and restore all functionality. Heal her from the top of her head to the soles of her feet." Then we chatted for about 10 minutes. I did not see Sally again for about 10 days.

When I saw her again, she told me she was back playing soccer in a few days with no pain in her knee. Then she asked me, "How did you know all those things about the meeting I was going to?" I realized that God had spoken through me as we chatted after I prayed for her knee. I could not recall what I had said in the conversation, so I said "I do not remember." I said, "Sally, I believe what occurred was God speaking to you in order to prepare you for the meeting you were called into." Sally stated that she had all the answers she needed for the surprise meeting they went to." God wants to prepare people for those surprise meetings so they will succeed. Sally told me that several hours after we chatted, her manager pulled her into an unplanned meeting. What God spoke to Sally through me gave her the information she needed for her manager. As a result, Sally impressed her manager and received a promotion.

On another occasion I was standing in the church lobby greeting people as they entered. As this couple walked past me, I felt God highlight them. At that time there was nothing more than my noticing them. I began to ponder why God had highlighted them to me for I had never met them before. As the service progressed God drew my attention to them two more times. I asked Holy Spirit, Lord, do you have something you want me to speak over them? As I did that, I saw a picture in my minds eye of them receiving something from God. These two people were in front of an ATM with their hands out to receive from the output slot of the ATM. When the service ended, I went over to the couple, introduced myself and said I feel I have a word from the Lord for you. I described what I saw and the word I believed the Lord wanted spoken. I asked them if this resonated with them. I allowed them to talk about the word for a few minutes then thanked them and moved on.

On another occasion I was speaking with some people visiting our church. As we conversed, I spoke out something that seemed odd. I told Suzie, not her real name that I saw her singing a song written by Debbie Boone. I told her what I saw and the word I felt the Lord wanted spoken from that picture. The person got very quiet and said, "How did you know that? That was the first song I ever sang." Through my obedience God touched Suzie bringing encouragement to her.

On another occasion I was doing some street ministry with my wife. As we spoke with a person who was looking in a bad way we asked if we could pray for him. He said "Yes." We then asked, "If you could receive a miracle what would you want? What would you want God to free you of?" He responded, "Nothing." I asked, "Would you like God to set you free from the cocaine addiction that keeps you living on the street?" He asked, "How do you know about my addiction?" I explained that "it was a word of knowledge, that God wants you to know that He knows how difficult your struggle is, that He wants to set you free." He got very quiet. I prayed for him that God would give him the desires of his heart, bringing freedom from issues that are holding him back.

In this example, as I drove to church; I prayed in tongues and spoke with Holy Spirit, asking that He move in the church service. The service began with us praising God. The worship team stayed on a song for a few minutes as they sensed something happening. I felt this word of prophecy well up from my belly. I said, "Many of you feel there are walls before you, behind you, beside you that you cannot get past. There is great power to defeat your enemies through worship. Give me your praise and watch as I cause those walls around you to fall." In this case I was prepared to deliver the word of prophecy by praying in tongues before the service. The power of praise will move the heart of God to act on our behalf.

The examples I have given show that God will prompt us in many different situations to speak for Him. It is key that we develop a close relationship with Holy Spirit where we communicate with Him through our day. As we walk in constant communication with Him we will be prepared for any situation that we encounter. God does not ask us to take on all the needs of this world ourselves. He does ask us to deal with those situations He speaks to us about. As we live our daily lives we need to be listening for His voice and what He is speaking to us. When we speak the word God gives us for others, there is impact, as great power is released to people in a very personal way.

Chapter 12

Including Wise Counsel

Where does wisdom come from and how does one apply it to their lives? We shall look at receiving wisdom, the benefits of wise counsel and incorporating this into the decisions of our daily lives.

Jesus said we are to be as wise as serpents, yet as innocent as doves (Matt 10:16). A key to being successful is to acquire and apply wisdom in our choices. Wisdom is the ability to discern or judge what is true, right, or lasting. Knowledge is information gained through experience, reasoning or acquaintance. One can know much information yet not be wise. Knowledge is having information on how to use a tool such as a power saw. Wisdom is knowing when to use it and when to keep it safely stored to protect others. Wisdom is a gift from God. "If any of you lacks wisdom, you should ask God, who gives generously to all without finding fault and it will be given to you" (James 1:5).

God gives us wisdom so we can glorify Him and understand how to use the knowledge He gives us. Knowledge would be knowing that the roads are covered with snow from the storm. Wisdom would direct us to wait for the snowplough to go by. If we had to drive before the road is ploughed, wisdom would say, drive slowly to avoid sliding into the ditch. In proverbs we read, "Plans fail for lack of counsel, but with many advisors they succeed" (Proverbs 15:22). We can draw on the experience, knowledge and good judgement of others to help us succeed. Through being teachable, we can be spared the pain of making the same mistakes others who went before us did. No person understands all things. We are created to need each other. As we discuss our decisions with trusted people we feel are wise, we can gain understanding from them.

"For those God foreknew He also predestined to be conformed to the image of His Son, that He might be the firstborn among many brothers and sisters" (Romans 8:29). Many people ponder their destiny. Destiny is the accumulation of events God has ordained to occur in the future. Predestined events are events determined by God's divine will in advance. The passage in Romans tells us that God has predestined us to be transformed into the image of His son Jesus. The events of this process will transpire over our lifetime on earth.

As we live our lives, we will see different points of transition. Some of these points are being born again, being water baptized, receiving the baptism of Holy Spirit, beginning to operate in the gifts of the spirit and moving into a new season with God. In each of these points of transition we made the decision to put action together with our faith. This journey is not a linear process but more of a winding road. How do we ensure we are making the right decision? We can become paralyzed with indecision at these crossroads, afraid of making the wrong decision. We should ask the Father for help to understand where He is leading us. As well, we should listen to input from people we trust. After speaking with God and other people, we need to put action with our belief. Even with the best counsel we can still make a wrong decision.

There will be times we will not know for certain that we are going in the correct direction until we look back some time later. We walk by faith and this is why we must rely upon God to direct us. Through this process it is important that we assess the direction in which we are going. Pay attention to that still small voice within you. Do you feel that something is not right? When I have gotten to points such as this, I stop, speak with Holy Spirit about what I am sensing. Then, I wait for Him to speak to hear what He has to tell me. If I am stifled by confusion, God will send someone to bring clarification to the situation. Also, I may have to battle spiritual forces of fear, doubt and uncertainty within myself through this process. Experience has shown me that I may need to make a decision to move forward and trust God for the outcome. As I step out in faith, He will confirm the direction or the next step I am to take. Momentum is better than paralysis.

As we walk out our days on earth, we can be vessels that Holy Spirit can touch others through. God moves us into the gifts incrementally. He gives us a measure of power to work with. As we are faithful to operate in this we will receive more. This way we learn to operate in the power of God without hurting other people. One learns to operate in the gift of prophesy in a similar manner.

To thrive, we follow the instructions God gave us. I make it my practice to keep short accounts with God. If I sin, I confess it quickly. Also, pray for those who have hurt us as directed in Scripture. I will say, Father I forgive the person who hurt me, I release them with no obligation to me. I ask that you would forgive them also. I bless them with everything you have for them in Jesus name. If I hurt someone I apologize and ask for forgiveness from the person and God.

Be mindful that discouragement is one of the devil's strategies to cause us to give up. Many times, I have come close to giving up. Feeling beaten up by people and circumstances, I would tell God I cannot do this. I would pour out my heart telling God why I could not go forward. When I stopped feeling sorry for myself, and asked for help, He was quick to help me. At first it would take me a few days to get my perspective back. As I have grown, the recovery time has gotten much shorter. As I returned to walking with God, I would repent of all the negative comments I made, as I spoke out of my pain. I would tell my Father, "I come out of agreement with the lies I have accepted and I come back into agreement with You."

Our own voice is the most powerful voice in our life, but there are times we need to be encouraged by another. Ask Holy Spirit to teach you to pray effective prayers. Look at Jesus example; He spoke the Word of God to the devil and defeated him. We should never speak with the devil, but speak to him, as we rebuke him.

There will be times we will be misunderstood. A good skill that will help us, is to keep our mouth shut when we are hurt. If we can avoid speaking from a place of not understanding things, we will avoid speaking unbelief. A good example of this is when the angel Gabriel came to Zechariah. Gabriel told Zechariah what was going to happen with Elizabeth having a son even though she was old. Zechariah began with questioning the angel about how this would happen which revealed his unbelief. The angel knowing that John the Baptist must be born did Zechariah a favour by closing his mouth for the next nine months. This favour prevented Zechariah from undermining God's plan with his words of doubt. The same works for us. If we can avoid speaking out of our pain, we can avoid undermining God's plan for our lives with doubt.

We are like military foot soldiers with little knowledge or ability to fight in battle. Through training and repetition, we become capable of battling the enemy with confidence. These exercises are done in the military over and over to teach the soldiers to respond without thinking. God takes us into His army and trains us to fight the enemy. He places us in situations where we will work through the techniques taught to us so we become more proficient in them. We give opportunity for problems to arise when we expect the battle, or the outcome, to be the way we feel it should be.

Offense comes when people do not respond as we think they should. We can derail relationships through taking offense. Jesus said, "The student is not above the teacher, nor a servant above his master" (Matthew 10:24). To be a disciple of Jesus, we need to be willing to accept unfair treatment that comes to us without being offended.

I have included some of my experience from which you may learn. Although I received mentoring, many of these questions were not satisfactorily answered in a way I could understand. To become a disciple of Jesus is to begin saying no to our wants and saying yes to God. Do not jump to the conclusion that God will ask you to give away all of your money, quit your job and move to an impoverished country tomorrow. However, do not rule out that He may ask you to do something radical. Give God opportunity to show you what He wants you to do. We do this as we ask Him to show us what He wants us to do, and then wait for Him to speak to us. As we do this we are acting in faith. When we say yes to God, He takes our words seriously. If you do, say the prayer I have included, expect Him to begin working in you to transform you into who He says you are. It is my experience that Holy Spirit will begin changing us one thing at a time. Since He is so efficient, changing that one thing or behaviour will cause other things in our lives to change.

As we embrace the process, He takes us through, we will grow closer to Him in relationship. Your life will be anything but boring. God's word tells us to test things, to ensure we are not deceived. This is called discernment, which is a characteristic of wisdom. Ongoing discernment is needed to determine if what a person speaks prophetically is from God.

When God created the New Testament church, He placed pastors in the church for a reason. It may be that your pastor is not embracing the gift of prophecy. Ask God to open their understanding to the great benefit prophecy is to the church. A big part of being a prophet is listening to Holy Spirit and doing what He tells you. Ask Holy Spirit if you are to stay or go from this church because you may be part of the solution.

Previously, I spoke about the law of lift that supersedes gravity. A pilot can get the plane to the end of the runway then sit there. If he does not follow the instructions to get the plane off the ground, he will remain at the end of the runway. He can remain stuck by believing a lie that gravity will not allow Him to take off. Similarly, we can believe lies about what is said in God's Word and miss out on the ability to walk with Him at a greater level of intimacy. If you are discontent with where you are in your walk with God and you want more, I am including a prayer of dedication for you. God takes the words of our mouth seriously. This is the kind of prayer God wants. Operating as a prophet flows out of our relationship with God. It requires we step out in faith flowing from our relationship with God. God will take us at our word where we are as we submit to Him. Choose to trust in God's love for you. He desires for you to walk in the gift of prophecy as a son or daughter of God. I encourage you to sincerely pray this prayer to your heavenly Father.

Father, I give all of me to You. Use every part of my life for Your kingdom. I will do whatever You want me to do. I will go anywhere You want me to go. I will say anything You want me to say. Father, I want the gift of prophecy. I submit myself to be used in any way You choose. Father, teach me what I need to change so that I can become a disciple of Jesus. I ask this in Jesus name, Amen.

The life of a prophet can be different from many others in this world. Take for example a bumblebee. The bumblebee has baffled many, including scientists in how it can fly. The size of the wings on the bumblebee appear to be too small for the size of body they have. Although this does not make sense to man's intellect, the bee flies without any issues. The design of God determines the outcome of all things and so the bumblebee flies. The bumblebee's self focus is to gather nectar from the flowers. As the bumblebee goes from flower to flower it gathers nectar. A by-product of the bee gathering nectar is that they cross-pollinate flowers. This is the bumblebee's communal purpose. Pollination is a necessary part of our food chain. Even though the bumblebee does not set out to cross pollinate the flowers they visit, this happens naturally. There is a larger scope to the created order as we see here.

Similarly, the main purpose for man on earth is to have fellowship with God. As we go through our day enjoying fellowship with God, we become a vessel for God to operate through. As this vessel, we can speak words from God that bring encouragement, exhortation and comfort to others. This is our communal purpose, to fulfill a larger plan.

Giving words of prophecy, is similar to providing water to dry land. In this world, a water hose is connected to a water supply. The hose will direct the flow of water to places of need, like gardens, lawns, watering cans, car wash, a thirsty person, etc. For the water to reach the required source the tap must be turned on. When it is, the water reaches the desired source, meeting the need it has.

In this world, we are the water hose, connected to Jesus, the source of life giving water. We are connected to Him through accepting Him as our Saviour. Holy Spirit is the tap that controls the flow of life giving words of prophecy through us. Through our relationship with Him, we hear the words He has for us to speak. By stepping out in faith, speaking these words, life-giving water is released to the recipients.

We are connected to the Father and Jesus through Holy Spirit. We must place importance upon our relationship with Holy Spirit. Holy

Spirit enables us to receive what the Father and Jesus have for us. The greater the priority we give relationship with Holy Spirit, the more fruitful our lives will be.

We are never too old to be used in the kingdom of God. As we get older we should have more wisdom to share with other people. As long as we have breath in our lungs, God can use us in this world to accomplish His goals. "In the last days, God says, I will pour out my Spirit on all people. Your sons and daughters will prophesy, your young men will see visions, your old men will dream dreams. Even on my servants both men and women, I will pour out my Spirit in those days and they will prophesy" (Acts 2:17-18). I believe we are in the days spoken about by this passage that was quoted from the prophet Joel by the apostle Peter. Do not let age or gender disqualify you from doing the work to which God has called you. If the church you are attending does not support you being involved in ministry, find a church that is moving with the Spirit of the living God. Do not become blind from following people who cannot see. Determine to be aligned with what Holy Spirit is doing where you can.

I will share with you some examples of how God has spoken to other people through me. These examples illustrate the ways God blessed the recipient of the word of prophecy and myself as the prophet.

I was at work in the washroom brushing my teeth when a co-worker came in. It is a funny thing, but God often speaks to me in the bathroom while brushing my teeth. I asked how his day was going. He explained that he bought a second house and needed to sell the existing house he owned. I listened to him speak for several minutes. As I did this, I heard the Lord tell me to tell him something. I questioned the Lord as I was taught not to give a word of prophecy with specific information. Again, I heard the Lord say, tell him. So, I looked at the person and said. You are going to sell your house this weekend and it will be to a person who has been through your house in the past two weeks. The person asked if I wanted to read their tea leaves as well. I replied, no thank you. This was Thursday and I was off until Monday. On Monday morning this same co-worker met me at work and began to ask, "How did you know that my house would be sold this weekend?" I went for a coffee with the person. I listened for the Lord and said what I felt He was speaking. I looked at the person and said, "I believe God gave me that word of knowledge to get your attention so you would listen to this. He loves you, your wife and family. He wants you to stop running and come home." The person sat there with a blank face and quiet for 20 or 30 seconds. Then he changed the subject and spoke about other matters. This word was accurate and an exception to what I was taught. Normally I would not give specific information about dates and people. In this case God showed me I could hear from Him clearly and He would honour His word even though it went against the way I was taught.

In another situation I gave a corporate word in a service. The word spoke directly to not listening to the devil and the lies he was speaking. "Look to me said the Lord and I will give you peace." Unknown to me people had been allowing a person to stay at their place. That weekend the person had ended their life. The word given was a real blessing to this family as God brought comfort to them that the person was in heaven with Him.

My last example took place in a service as it was beginning. We had sung a worship song and the worship team asked us to greet each other. As I did a man came into the service. As He did, I felt the presence of Holy Spirit increase around me. I felt God tell me to let him know this. So, I went back to him and said, "As you came into this service, I felt the presence of Holy Spirit increase significantly. You are carrying much more of God's Glory than you may recognize." This man later told me that he had been through a tough two weeks and that word was a great encouragement to him.

May your life be like the bumblebee that brings beauty and wonder to many in this world. The bumblebee defies all logic as it flies. May you be used of God to defy what people think you could never do. The bee is not limited in flying because of what we comprehend. No, the bee flies in spite of what we do not understand. I pray that your life shall be likewise. As you go about your daily activities be someone God operates through in spite of what others think is possible. May you grow to become a prophet through whom God speaks and communicates His love to those in your sphere of influence.

Gaining and applying wisdom can protect us from many hardships.

Applying wisdom when interpreting a word of prophecy, will help us to receive the benefit of the word the Lord spoke to us.

Summary

As a believer in Jesus Christ, we live our lives on earth in rich fellowship with God as our goal, and heaven as our final destination. We are running the race set before us as we live our daily lives. As we have discovered, all can prophesy. The choices we make in our lives will determine where we go with God. Are you experiencing thoughts stirred up in your heart from reading this book? I encourage you to write these thoughts down and ask God to help you process them. Similar to how ground is tilled before planting, Holy Spirit will till the soil of our hearts to bring new growth. Things in the soil of our hearts must be stirred up to birth them or remove them accordingly. This can occur regularly, as needed in different seasons or times of our lives.

Some things in the soil of our heart must be removed for the God seeds to grow. As a field is tilled, rocks are stirred up and must be removed before planting. Our hearts may be stony and hard. Our hearts may need to be tilled to bring to the surface what must be birthed or removed. Make the decision to give Holy Spirit permission to till your heart. He has great plans for you. Run to God, ask Him bold questions of what you are to do. He is for you and He will help you. Give Holy Spirit permission to take hold of your life and orient you according to His plan. He wants you to accomplish the call of God on your life more than you do.

Intentionally embrace the work Holy Spirit is doing in your life right now. Decide today that you will remain engaged in the process He has for you each day. As we go through the process every part of our flesh will scream to give up when it gets hard. This is understandable.

Getting to our destiny is done one decision at a time. When Jesus asks you to do something, say yes and do what He asks. He is not looking for perfection, but for a person who is willing to try. Attaining the goal can be as simple as that. Each time Jesus asks you to do something, say yes and do it.

Submission and obedience are keys to moving forward with the Lord. We will not go anywhere as a disciple until we choose to obey what Jesus asks us to do. We must accept and live by this truth. Holy Spirit is for us and wants us to achieve God's plan for our life. We hear the Word of God, we speak the Word of God and we read the Word of God. But, do we believe the Word of God? Do we 'Do' the word of God? Scripture tells us that all can prophesy. The word "all" includes you. This means that 'you' can prophesy!

This book has addressed foundational truths required to get you started. God wants us as children of God to represent Him in this world. We represent Jesus as we operate in the gift of prophecy. I have personally seen prophesy operate like a key into a person's heart, bypassing many intellectual barriers to unlocking things in their innermost being. God reaches all of His children through this dynamic grace gift.

So, what is the first step? If you are feeling confused, may I suggest you take some time to sit and listen to what Holy Spirit is telling you. Allow God to speak through other trusted people to help you understand what He is speaking. Then be intentional to act upon what He tells you to do. Decide now that you will not allow what others might think to stop you from obeying what Jesus asks you to do.

Do you find yourself hesitant to step out wondering what certain people will think of you? Do you talk your self out of giving a prophetic word? Do you say things like, I do not have the full word? What will the pastor say if I mess it up? Allowing these thoughts to control you is walking in fear.

A plane can be fully fuelled and ready for takeoff but still requires one thing to leave the ground. It requires intentional action by the pilot. As the pilot goes through the takeoff procedure including throttling up the engines, the plane will begin moving forward. Similarly, in our lives we will take off when our actions intentionally obey what God tells us to do. Listen to Holy Spirit, do what He tells you to do. Throttle up your engines as you step out in faith. This will create the thrust needed to propel you forward into what you are called to do.

As a plane takes off it flies directly into the wind to get maximum lift. This is opposite to what we would think is correct. It would seem logical that the plane would use the wind to push it as it accelerates. When it has left the ground and reached the required speed, the pilot will correct the direction of travel according to the planned destination.

Similarly, as we step out in the direction we believe God is calling us to go, we will encounter resistance. God will use the opposition we face to give us greater lift. This is an example of how things happen opposite to how we think they should. It would seem that the plane would use the wind blowing it forward to gain greater speed for take off, yet the opposite is true. In God many things are also different than we understand. We need to learn how God uses forces against us to work for us. Believing this is an act of faith. After you have taken a step of faith, He will adjust your direction of travel so you get to where you are intended to be.

You have read about exploring the gift of prophecy. This will enable you to begin operating with a level of proficiency. I encourage you to pursue God for what you need to begin to operate in this gift. Step out in faith engaging the thrust of God to propel you forward. He is waiting for you to take that step of faith. Father, I bless every person who reads this book that they will be able to move forward into a greater place with You. I ask that You will give them understanding to recognize the place in their lives requiring change. I ask you to help them let go of their plans and embrace Your plans, Amen.

It has been my experience growing as a prophet that God's grace is always available for the journey. I have often seen God's pleasure when a spoken word has brought encouragement to another person. Like a father that delights in his children learning something new, it is similar with us and God as we grow in this gift. Trust that God is able to use you as a powerful messenger speaking words of encouragement, exhortation and comfort as a prophet.

Recommended Reading

The Voice of God – How God speaks personally and corporately to His children today. Cindy Jacobs

Good morning Holy Spirit – Bennie Hinn

Battlefield for the Mind – Joyce Meyer

Hearing the voice of God – Dr. Mark Virkiler

Thank You

Thank you for choosing to read my book. I thank you for taking the time to read and benefit from the book content. If this book has been a benefit to you, would you take time to write a review on Amazon.com. In doing this you support me as the author and make others aware of this book that can benefit them.

Yours,

Steve Condon

Biography

My life was typical of one born into a large Catholic family that promoted hard work as the way to get ahead in life. My parents spoke about God, yet I did not know God. I felt there was a God, yet had no concept of relationship with God. It seemed that my interactions with God were driven by traditions rather than intimacy. When I was 21 my life changed forever. I came to know God in a very personal way. My life came to a crossroads. In my need, I called out to Jesus, asking for His help. As weak as my moment of repentance was, Jesus honoured it becoming Lord of my life. This experience placed me on a journey of discovering relationship with God that has continued since that moment. As a passionate person, I pour myself into what I believe in. Today, my passion is to raise up people in the gift of prophecy, so they will be a vessel God will speak through, blessing people everywhere.

About 18 months ago, the Lord asked me to write a book. This thought seemed random and perplexed me greatly. I contemplated how I would be able to write a book about prophecy. How does one speak about the communications of an eternal God through words of prophecy? For several weeks after God asked me, I said nothing for I felt what I heard was not from God. Why would God ask me to create a manuscript when I was not a writer? When I shared what God had asked me to do with my wife Colleen, she affirmed this was likely God's leading.

As I embarked on this project, I decided to do my very best to accomplish writing this manuscript. I invited Holy Spirit into the process. As I looked for His leading, He led me through the many parts of completing this project. It was a huge leap of faith into the unknown. This journey began with an invigorating dialogue and experience with Holy Spirit. At times I felt very vulnerable, unequipped to create a book. This process has redefined what I understood to be true about God and has deepened my relationship with Him. You can follow me on face book at facebook.com/stevecondonauthor/

Workbooks are available for separate purchase. For information on how to schedule Steve for speaking sessions, send inquiries by email to SteveCondon57@gmail.com

10081707R00066

Manufactured by
Amazon.ca
Bolton, ON